ARMCHAIR
REAL ESTATE
MILLIONAIRE

BAZINGA Publishing

www.armchairrealestatemillionaire.com

ISBN: 978-1-7774094-1-8 (print)
ISBN: 978-1-7774094-2-5 (ebook)

Ordering Information:
Special discounts are available on quantity purchases by corporations, associations, and others. For details, contact bazinga@ArmchairRealEstate.com

This book is dedicated to all of the dreamers, who imagine more and want to live their best life. They want more wealth, more success, more choices and more freedom.

ARMCHAIR
REAL ESTATE
MILLIONAIRE

IF YOU'RE SITTING THERE ANYWAY, YOU MIGHT AS WELL BUILD YOUR WEALTH

MICHAEL DOMINGUEZ

TABLE OF CONTENTS

CHAPTER 1

GETTING STARTED

You all know the question adults ask kids, "What do you want to be when you grow up?" You would always get the usual answers, like a policeman, fireman, teacher, etc. I wanted to be a millionaire.

Fast forward into my mid-twenties and I meet a girl, get married, have a son, get a "responsible" job, and get promoted a couple of times. Before you know it I'm in upper-middle management in a retail organization, with a mortgage, other debts, few savings, and well into the rat race.

I remember thinking, How the hell did that happen?

I went through a lot of bumps to figure it out and reach the success I have today and we'll get back to that story, but what I want you to know now is: **You don't have it all figured out on day 1 or even day 101.**

Chances are by the time you've picked up this book, you've had some success in other ventures. Maybe you've built up a little cash. Perhaps you now have some equity in your home. You're building a decent career. Regardless, you're ready to move forward and take the next steps on your path to financial freedom.

Over the years, my mentors provided me with a lot of advice and coaching that have brought me where I am today. I feel that it is my responsibility to pass along that knowledge, with my own take on it, to the next generation of real estate investors. I'm honored that you're taking time to invest in yourself and are using my teachings as a part of that. I don't claim that any of the lessons in this book are new and original, but perhaps a little easier to comprehend through my interpretation.

I WANT YOU TO THINK OF THIS BOOK AS A ROAD MAP FOR FINANCIAL SUCCESS.

I was never mistaken for the smartest kid in the class. My grades were consistently in the bottom half. In fact, there would not even be a top half of student grades if it wasn't for people like me.

My goals were pretty simple. I wanted to build a portfolio of quality investment properties, all with positive cash flow and in geographic locations prime for appreciation. I wanted to add an investment property to my portfolio every year for 10 straight years. As an investment Realtor, I wanted to be the best and most knowledgeable I could be.

Over this past decade, I have been able to meet both my investing and Realtor goals. It is with these years of learning and taking action that I share my path with you.

This road map will help you buy two or three residential homes in quality neighborhoods, where you can attract quality tenants and receive quality rents, which will, in turn, make you quality profits. Wealth building doesn't have to be a full-time job, be full of risk, or be overly complicated.

My investment strategy looks a lot like the tortoise in the old tortoise and the hare fable. I advocate purchasing just one property and getting that one running smoothly, and possibly the following year buying a second one. If you can do that for three straight years, manage those properties, and hold on to them, then you have set the wheels in motion for your retirement.

A good road map should have a method that just about anyone can follow. One that once you read the "instructions," you think it is almost too easy.

Different investors will be at different parts of their journey, so you can find information under the following buckets:

1. What you should Look for In your Properties: Chapters Two through Four

2. How to finance: Chapters Four through Eight

3. Managing your properties: Chapter Nine through Fourteen

You'll be able to use this road map throughout your real estate investment journey. As you develop your portfolio, you'll likely revisit a lease or structure a joint venture for properties in the future. You do not need to take in the whole process at once, but take it one step at a time.

We have all seen the stats. As Andrew Carnegie said more than a century ago, more than 90 percent of the world's millionaires got there in large part because of their real estate holdings. That statement was true in his time just as much as it is true today. I know this sounds overly simplistic, but how do you catch a lot of fish? Well . . . you find a spot where the fish are.

How do you become wealthy? Well ...you find a spot where all the wealthy people are.

CHAPTER 2

THE GOLDILOCKS PRINCIPLE

"There is no downside to a side hustle. There are only benefits to building more than one source of income. A side hustle is the new job security."
—Forbes

We all know the story of "Goldilocks and the Three Bears." You can debate whether or not Goldilocks should have been charged for breaking and entering, but I'm not going to address that here. In the story, Goldilocks is repeatedly faced with three options to choose from and in each scenario has to determine the one that's "just right" for her.

As I will continue to say, the investors who build truly sustained "generational wealth" are the ones that hold on to their assets, not just for a couple of years, but for life. Yes, you can make some quick cash doing flipping, wholesaling, and other short-term projects. But besides being a lot of work, there is an element of risk involved that I would rather avoid.

I am a "buy and hold" investor. I always aim to talk others out of selling their assets unless it makes more sense to divest themselves of that asset because they can use the funds for assets they now prefer. It is fair to review your portfolio every year or so to determine if you would still buy this property today if you had the chance. If the answer is "hell no," then you might then consider moving on.

When deciding what you want to invest in, perhaps consider this. Before you buy, think about what kind of tenant you want to have and then find a property that will attract that tenant.

It seems that nearly every real estate book tells you that you only make money on the buy. Don't get me wrong; I am in favor of getting a good price, just as much as anyone else. However, there are times I might have to pay "market value" for a great property in a great location. I might as well attract a tenant who will want to live there. If that property was in a market with strong fundamentals, I am comfortable saying I will be pleased with its "market value" in 10 years' time. The key is to hold on to that asset for 10 years.

But I'm getting ahead of myself. What options does Goldilocks have to choose between when placing her investment dollars? There are four main types of residential investing and the tenant profile varies based on which path you choose.

SINGLE-FAMILY HOMES AND CONDOS

A single-family rental can be a freehold detached, semi-detached, townhouse home, or a condo, whether that be in a building or perhaps in a townhome community. The type of tenant that goes along with this type of rental is typically the easiest to manage. If you have a nicely renovated home in a good location, you can expect to find a tenant who will respect your property. A well-maintained home should not require much day-to-day management.

These properties can attract the best tenants available in the market. Sometimes, tenants rent not because they can't afford to purchase a home in that market, but because they simply prefer to rent. Perhaps they will only be in that city for a few years; perhaps they had some spotty credit in the past or have non-verifiable income (such as some self-employed people) and can't qualify for a mortgage right now; perhaps a divorced parent wants to stay in a school district, but needed to sell their house; perhaps a new immigrant has great income but no credit history in North America. Regardless, these tenants can be fantastic to work with.

The downside of owning this asset class is that the monthly cash flow may be minimal or even negative. If there is a repair required or a vacancy, the cash flow for the year is essentially wiped out.

Let me go into more detail about cash flow. Think of your rental property as a business. The rental income is the revenue that comes into your business. Your expenses can be broken down into two categories: fixed and variable expenses.

Fixed expenses are your mortgage payments, municipal taxes, and property insurance. An investor can't just stop paying for any of those things. Even if the property is vacant for a month—and it will be at some point—these fixed expenses keep occurring.

Variable expenses are ones that will occur, but not every month. Repairs and maintenance are good examples of a variable expense. You may not have a repair every month, but any homeowner knows that at some point, something will break down. Also, there are preventative things like furnace filters, cleaning gutters, and improving the grading of the yard. These are situations when nothing is actually broken, but by spending a little bit now, you'll prevent major repair costs down the road.

Other variable expenses include property management and vacancy allowance. Initially, you can do property management work yourself, especially if you have just a couple of properties. However, as your portfolio grows, your need for outside help also grows. You could make the case that property owners with just one property should absolutely have a property manager who will keep up on the legal rules and regulations, but in reality, very few single-property landlords actually do that.

Vacancy allowance is a tricky one to account for. It is not a true expense, but actually a lack of revenue for a period of time. Regardless, it's important to have a reserve in place for the variable expenses that pop up. Note that I don't count utilities as expenses. Tenants should pay the actual cost of the utilities themselves, whether they are in the tenant's name or the owner's name.

Anyone can justify the purchase of an investment property with negative cash flow by saying that they can cover the hundreds of dollars in overages, thus allowing the buyer to add the property into their portfolio. They compare the "expense" of negative cash flow to putting their money into a monthly drip campaign to purchase equities such as stocks or mutual funds. The rationality is that the shortfall in revenue is just the cost of doing business, and the property will be worth more in a few years.

I want all my properties to—at minimum—cover their expenses shortly after I acquire them. If I am unable to work my "nine-to-five" job for whatever reason, I want to know that my assets can take care of themselves.

In fact, I want them to actively help me out every month. The concern I have with negative cash flow properties is that if things go sideways and you don't have the funds to supplement the property each month, the only viable solution is to sell that asset. The problem with this is that it may not be an ideal time to sell that asset. Is the market also sideways? Is there an international pandemic and the entire real estate market is in turmoil? Will there be a huge expense to break the mortgage? If you are in a dire situation, you may not have a choice. A positive cash flow property allows you to ride out the stormy weather of a market downturn.

Finally, even if you have the wherewithal to withstand a market down turn with a negative cash flow property, these types of properties are PORTFOLIO KILLERS. Lenders take all your income and expenses when evaluating whether you can be "awarded" another mortgage. If you have negative cash flow properties in your portfolio, this will hurt your chances of getting another mortgage and building that portfolio.

As much as Goldilocks likes the tenant profile of the single-family home, the negative cash flow is too much to take on. Since Goldilocks wants to build her portfolio large enough that she can meet her net wealth and cash flow goals, as much as she might like them, single-family rentals just aren't right for her. My advice to Goldilocks would be to keep looking for an alternative option.

MULTIUNIT BUILDINGS

A multiplex of four or more units can earn cash flow very well. In most cases, there is one heat source, one roof, and one lot. In this property, you can generate multiple rents and minimize negative cash flow risk if one property is vacant, under repair, or the tenant simply isn't paying. Multiple rents can mitigate that risk.

Goldilocks likes the idea of owning a building. When she tells the story of her investment portfolio, she likes the idea of pointing to a real building and saying, "That one is mine." She imagines how impressed her family and friends will all be when she opens up her phone and scrolls through the photos of the building(s) she owns. Owning the whole building can make you look very successful.

Financing a multi, however, can be a whole different challenge. Often, these properties fall under a commercial mortgage, with higher interest rates, a larger percentage down payment required, a much higher purchase price, and a whole bunch more paperwork. The lenders ask for EVERYTHING. Sometimes two or three times, in fact. We recently refinanced a nineplex that took nearly nine months to complete. When dealing with commercial lenders, you need patience and perseverance.

When it comes to lending, remember the GOLDEN RULE: he who holds the gold, makes the rules. It's easy to forget that when you're trying to secure financing on a really good opportunity. It seems more and more that prior banking history and relationships with that lender don't matter that much to them. They put all the information into a computer, an algorithm does its thing, and then the computer spits out the verdict on whether or not they should take on that mortgage.

The good news with commercial lending is that the lenders look far more heavily at the strength of the asset itself rather than at the strength of the borrower, but there are simply SO many more hoops to jump through in order to obtain that mortgage. Often, the lender will ask for environmental conditions of the property; verification with the city of the legality of the units; detailed information of each existing tenant; detailed breakdown of the heat source, electricals, plumbing—and the condition of each; fire safety certificates; and so much more.

Multiunits can allow the property owner to multiply their wealth growth—and reach their financial freedom goals that much quicker— as the larger property receives more income than a single-family home, and therefore pays off more debt.

But the thing that scares this Goldilocks off multiunit buildings is not only the onerous lending rules, but also the tenant profile. Apartment renters are simply different from single-family home renters. It may feel like a stereotype, but a renter in a home more often treats the home as their own. The more renovated it is, the more likely the tenant will care for the home. There really is a direct correlation. But multiplex tenants tend to be more transactional. Especially in inner-city and inner-town multiunit complexes, these are often not future property owners. It is a very different landlording experience.

Goldilocks may decide to solicit a property manager (PM) to handle tenant issues, such as conflicts, vacancies, tenant placements, missed rent payments, and did I mention conflicts? There are a number of quality property management companies available across the country. However, even a good PM can only do so much. Also, keep in mind that they charge a fee for their services, which will eat away at your cash flow. Appointing a PM is certainly not a case of "set it and forget it." If you contract out management of the building, you must still manage the PM to ensure that things are not being missed.

CASE STUDY
ANYONE WANT A COUCH?

I often joke that I should open a store offering used couches left behind by departing tenants. They are often scratched by pets, have broken toys in the cushions, and are in pretty rough shape overall. But the worst by far was one couch left behind by a female tenant. Her boyfriend had a skin disorder that made his skin regularly flake and, essentially, shed off. After the tenant left, the carpet and the couch were practically white with dead skin. I think I had to pay the workers extra to carry that one down the stairs.

If you want to make a real estate investor chuckle, tell them that real estate is passive income. That's how it is classified for taxes, of course. But being a real estate property owner is very much a job. It is a business. It requires regular attention, just like any other business that you might own, or side hustle you may take on. Being an "Armchair Millionaire" doesn't mean totally hands-off investing. In my real estate seminars, I often tell the crowd, "It's a part-time job that can make you a millionaire." But it is by no means passive. No, you don't have to be at the office or factory each day when owning real estate, but you do have to manage the building and the land/property (or at minimum manage the property manager). The larger the property, it seems, the more things can go wrong. And those things cost a lot more than in the single-family home.

The choice of location of a multiunit is often less flexible, too. The best cash-flowing multiunit buildings typically already exist and may be 40-plus years old. The current property owner may not maintain the property like you would, so expect to inherit some (or a lot of) deferred maintenance if you buy an established property.

The building may also not be in an area of town where you would want to live. Yeah, it is true that "everyone has to live somewhere," but if you have a target tenant profile, even if you renovate your property to the best of your ability, it may be in a sketchier neighborhood. So even if you can attract your target tenant, they could still move on because they don't like the community. You are then left with your pick of the "B"- and "C"-quality tenants.

The goal, as I have said, is to HOLD an asset for at least 10 years. Despite the superior cash flow projections, many multiunit property owners choose to sell off their buildings earlier than this. The most common reasons I hear are that they didn't make the cash flow they thought they would make because expenses kept popping up, or they were sick and tired of dealing with crappy and potentially confrontational tenants.

Finally, if you're still thinking of selling before the 10-year goal, remember how hard it was for you to get that mortgage. Let's assume that you were able to build some forced appreciation into the building, plus the values in the community have also gone up. Well, now there are simply FAR fewer potential buyers that can afford a multiunit building than that single-family home. That doesn't mean you can't find a buyer. Just remember that it may take months or even years to sell a multiunit building, especially if you bought that property in a market with mediocre market fundamentals. We will discuss market fundamentals in the next chapter.

My advice to Goldilocks is to think long and hard before buying a multiunit building. But if she wants to proceed, she should make sure she has a great team of contractors, property management, paralegals, and more before making that purchase.

COMMERCIAL OR MIXED-USE BUILDINGS

The biggest advantage of the commercial tenant is that this type of tenancy doesn't fall under the landlord/tenant act in most provinces and states. This means the rules are often more advantageous to the landlord. If the tenant doesn't pay, you have the right to kick them out and change the locks.

Another advantage is that, as landlord, you can negotiate to have the tenant not just pay rent and utilities for the space, but you can also include in the lease something called CAM fees. These are common area maintenance fees such as snow removal, property maintenance, parking lot maintenance, roof repair, and more. Let's say a plaza has 10,000 square feet of usable retail or commercial space, and one unit is 1,000 square feet. The tenant for that unit is responsible for 10 percent of the CAM fees for the time they lease that premises. One other advantage is that the same tenant could also be responsible for 10 percent of the municipal property taxes.

As landlord, you are essentially only responsible for debt financing. A landlord of a fully tenanted commercial building or plaza, with leases stipulating the tenants pay all the CAM fees, has very few day-to-day expenses that they can't pass on to the tenants.

As great as that sounds, I advise you to think long and hard about acquiring this type of property. There are buildings and plazas across North America that have had vacancies for years.[1] I still see vacant units in decently located plazas once occupied by big-name video stores, department stores, or restaurant chains. These premium plazas have had a real challenge refilling these units.

The downtown storefronts across the country are having an even harder time. If you are old enough, you may recall a time when downtown was a happening place on weekends.[2] You would do all of your shopping downtown. Do you remember the last time you had a major shopping trip downtown? In the 1960s and '70s, customers left the downtown area for the convenience of the shopping mall or the suburban plaza.

Downtown landlords have had to adjust to this shift in customer preferences by renting to restaurants, tattoo parlours, and discount retailers. But across many downtown areas there are a lot of long-term vacancies. In the residential world, landlords cry when they go two months without a paying tenant. Imagine a commercial building, which can go two years without rental income. Sure, in some cases the area is vibrant and full of people. But as you drive down Main Street USA, there are a lot of vacant units.

All of this is without the fallout from the 2020 economic shutdown. There will be some plazas and malls that never recover from the effects of COVID-19.[3]

I personally spent more than 15 years in the world of retail management. I was involved in lease negotiations with landlords across Ontario, Canada. I understand the benefits and the risks of commercial real estate. The way people shopped in the 1950s differed greatly from how they shopped in the 1980s. That, in turn, differs greatly from how people shop in the 2020s. How many people do you know who do 25 percent or more of their shopping online today? Do you think that trend will continue? Will online shopping likely represent an even higher percentage of the way people shop in years to come?

In some cities today, once prosperous malls and plazas are now like ghost towns, with lights turned off, abandoned fixtures, and broken signs of defunct businesses.[4] The "big boy" investors of commercial space are looking for alternative ways to generate revenue. Some are even tearing down old, tired malls and plazas and reusing that space for residential or even self storage.

Let's look at the financing aspect of purchasing this type of building. Besides needing a very large down payment that will likely be out of reach for many individual investors, interest rates are often much higher and the down payment percentage required will be greater, because of the inherent risk involved in owning this type of property. Lenders typically only offer a shorter amortization, making the monthly payments that much higher. They want the property owner to have a much larger amount of "skin in the game."

For our young investor, Goldilocks, this investment class is just out of her league. The amount of down payment cash required, along with the risks associated with owning her own retail plaza (even if it has some residential units to supplement the income) are just not for her.

As a risk-averse investor, I want to stay away from being on the wrong side of a trend. I know that residential real estate isn't going anywhere anytime soon. People are going to want to live in the properties I own in 20 years, especially if I bought in an area that is well located with transit, shopping, and employment.

TWO-UNIT DWELLING, DUPLEX, OR ADDITIONAL DWELLING UNIT

This investment class can offer a similar cash flow per door of a multiplex with the tenant profile of the single-family dwelling. Some premium tenants will not like the idea of "sharing a house" with another tenant but if your place is the nicest on the market and priced 20 percent below the single-family home rentals, you won't have a vacancy for too long.

As you will see in the final chapter, there is a trend in cities across North America advocating for some densification in their communities. A potential investor can make their choice of location within the town or city. In many markets, you can convert your home into a two-unit suite (or secondary suite). The neighbors maintain their yards and most homes look great. Because you are choosing where to create this home, you can select a quiet street, but close to shopping or public transit.

In the upcoming chapters, I'll be discussing the importance of creating legal secondary suites. Part of the research required in determining a market you want to invest in will be what that community's rules are in the alliance of secondary suites. In Chapter 13, The Missing Middle, we will talk about the many benefits of encouraging secondary suites in your community. However, not all city leaders feel the same way, and assuming you can't change the policy of that community, it's best that you take your investment dollars to a community that wants you to invest there and wants to see a growing pool of safe, legal, renovated, affordable housing in their neighborhoods.

Some communities have a strong inventory of desirable properties available for purchase for conversion to a two-unit suite. These "turnkey" properties are essentially ready to go. You can buy this property, turn the key, and it's all set for renting. But most properties in this category will require you to go through the process to legalize it for secondary suite status by meeting the building and fire codes, along with any municipal bylaws. There is absolutely a learning curve in purchasing and renovating these properties, but once completed, they are highly desirable rentals that can generate far more rental income than had the home been left as a single-family home.

I often say that if it were that easy, everyone would do it. It is not the easiest path to take but it is something you can learn. It is somewhat predictable. It is repeatable.

More good news about this investment class is that by creating an additional legal suite, the owner has added market value to her property. In the event that she ever wanted to sell the property, a legal secondary suite will be highly sought after by both investors and multi-generational families.

Investors can also refinance the property after the renovation is complete. It will often be appraised at a higher value than neighboring homes because of the renovation. This refinanced money can be used to pay down expenses incurred during the renovation or can go toward the acquisition of future properties. In fact, the added rental income will make it easier to quality for future properties. Plus, because it is a legal secondary suite, most lenders will take the income from both units and use that for the mortgage-qualifying process.

Certainly, strong cash flow properties are self-sustaining. Even if we encounter a real estate market correction, remember, once you own the property, you don't really care what the real estate market is doing. You are more focused on the rental market. Often, during tougher economic times, as more people can't afford homes, rental demand and rental prices actually rise. As long as you aren't looking to sell your investment, does it really matter what the market conditions may be in the short-term future?

This all brings us back to Goldilocks and her dilemma of where to put her investment dollars. She wants the cash flow of each property, she wants it in a good condition, and she doesn't want to be dealing with a slew of problem tenants. She wants a property that doesn't take over her life and is manageable with just a few hours a month overseeing her investment. Goldilocks, therefore, feels that investing in two-unit homes is "Just Right!"

You must either modify your dreams, or magnify your skills.
—Jim Rohn

 # ARMCHAIR MINDSET PLAYBOOK

- Monthly cash flow is what's left after all of the variable and fixed expenses are subtracted from the rental income.

- The tenant profile of the multi-unit building can be less desirable. The location might be a little sketchy too.

- Mixed use and commercial buildings can have long term vacancies and might be too hard for the newer investor.

- Single family homes and condos should be able to deliver the ideal tenant, but doesn't offer the desired cash flow.

- Two-Unit dwellings & Duplexes can deliver on tenant profile, cash flow and location.

CHAPTER 3

LEGALIZED INSIDER TRADING

"One thing we can all control is effort. Put in the time to become an expert in whatever you're doing. It will give you an advantage because most people don't do this."
—Mark Cuban, American entrepreneur and investor

C an we count on our employer or our government to be there for us when we approach our senior years? If history has shown us anything, it's that the people who take their financial future into their own hands get further ahead. Employers are doing everything in their power to avoid committing to a lifelong pension for their former employees. If you look back at the largest employers from just 50 years ago, how many of them don't even exist anymore?[5, 6]

As for North America, the annual deficit and the overall national debt offer me little confidence that their governments will even be in a position to be there for me in 20–30 years. At the time of this writing, Canadian debt has reached $763 billion and US debt is over $26 trillion (yes, trillion!). Both governments are experiencing record annual deficits in 2020.[7, 8]

I don't think you will find many people out there who are truly counting on some employer or government pension plan as their sole retirement source. So why is it that, according to a recent study by GoBankingRates, about 42 percent of Americans are at risk of retiring broke, with less than $10,000 saved for retirement?[9]

The best way to break the cycle is to spend a little time on your financial education. I find it amusing that those that claim they have no time to educate themselves could then share with you all the things that are wrong with their local sports team, the goings on with the top reality TV show of the day, political debates, or the happenings of the Hollywood stars. I can assure you that the Kardashians, LeBron James, and Donald Trump don't pay attention to your financial future. Maybe you can carve out 10 percent of the time you spend on their affairs and spend it on your own.

By understanding the market fundamentals, you can become the ultimate market insider.

HERE ARE SOME FAMOUS REAL ESTATE MYTHS

- Real estate values always go up!
- It's a good deal because it's cheap!
- You only make money on the buy!
- If property values do drop, they will bounce back!

Not all real estate is created equal. In a perfect world, we would have unlimited amounts of equity and unlimited ability to obtain credit, which would let us buy anything we want. But we know that's not reality.

We need to make some smart choices. In the game show Let's Make a Deal, contestants must choose between doors number one, two, and three. For real estate investors, there are way more choices than that. How do you know what the best choice is?

Because I still haven't been able to turn a DeLorean into a time machine, I can't know for sure what the future will hold. The good news for us is that we can look at certain indicators which give us suggestions of where the growth will be most prominent.

Becoming an expert might sound like a lot of work, but it is possible.

The great news is that once you find the right market, unless something major affects that community, that area should remain a highly desirable place to invest. If you choose someday to expand your portfolio, the skilled investor can return to their armchair as they oversee their "empire."

THE LONG-TERM REAL ESTATE SUCCESS FORMULA

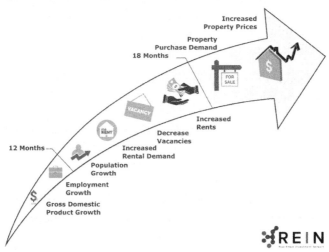

REIN's Long-Term
Real Estate Success Formula

Increased
Property Prices

Property
Purchase Demand

18 Months

Increased
Rents

Decrease
Vacancies

12 Months

Increased
Rental Demand

Population
Growth

Employment
Growth

Gross Domestic
Product Growth

REIN

The Canadian Real Estate Investment Network (REIN) has created "The Long-Term Real Estate Success Formula." Why recreate a system when others before us have dissected a system that works so well? REIN and the Success Formula helped to create the formula that I use to this day, both for myself and to teach others. For anyone looking at enhancing their knowledge, I can tell you that the REIN group is worth the investment of your time and your money.

Not all markets are the same. I realize it is not a revelation that Detroit real estate values are lower than those found in Los Angeles. But why? Also, since Detroit values are so cheap, does this mean it is a good opportunity?

There is no reason to guess! Let's look at the market fundamentals to determine future values.

The first thing to look at when determining a quality market is that market's **Gross Domestic Product Growth**. Is the GDP (in that market) growing, slowing, or staying the same? We are not as interested in short-term blips as much as long-term trends in that market.

The cool thing is, unlike 20-plus years ago, this data isn't all that hard to obtain. Simply starting your search by googling GDP growth in your city of choice should get you the data you need. If you are curious to know the fastest-growing cities in the US, search GDP growth by US city. With little exception, the cities growing the quickest are located in warm-weather states like Texas, Florida, Arizona, Nevada, California, and the Carolinas.

You might think, what exactly is GDP and why is it so important? A reasonable definition might be:

The total value of goods produced and services provided in a country or market during one year.

OK. It is interesting to know what that number might be, but what really helps us to determine the quality of a market is whether that number is growing and if so, by how much?

But dive a little deeper. If the market is growing, why is that happening? On a national or even a state or provincial level, it might be tough to get a handle on the reason. But in one city or town, a few good things can really make a difference. Did some new companies enter the market? Improved transit and roadways allowing companies to ship more products to their customers? What's going on in the community that you are studying and, most importantly, is the reason for that growth sustainable?

What often combines quickly with GDP growth is **Job Growth**: in other words, the number of people employed in any given market. This makes sense. If businesses are busier, they will need to hire more people to service that increase in business. Most of the time, the surge in employment growth will initially come from the pool of job seekers already living near the employer. You will see rises in the city's employment rate. But if the growth is sustained, you will see employers look beyond the local community to hire people. Those employees may need to relocate.

As they say in the movie Field of Dreams, "If you build it he [they] will come." In this case build the employment opportunities, and the people will come. This means **Population Growth**.

Now, these people need to live somewhere. History has shown that when new employees transfer to a new market, they choose to rent their residence, not buy. This may be because they cannot qualify for a mortgage or they simply aren't sure whether they will be staying and where they would want to own that property. Nonetheless, there is an **Increased Rental Demand** that comes from population growth.

It is often reported by the media that rental amounts are simply too high. This data often comes out of studies that compare rental rates from prior decades with today's and suggest that this rate of increase is unsustainable for the average employee. On one hand that statement is correct. It's true that many employees will be priced out of the rental market and will have to locate far outside of that market and commute into town in order to work.[10, 11] The reality though, is that if the property owner placed an unreasonable value on the monthly rental rate, he simply wouldn't be able to find a tenant. So, what happens next on the Success Formula trajectory is **Decreased Vacancies**.

The rental market prices are set by the market's supply and demand forces. That means the prices of rentals today reflect a balance of the amount of supply of places to rent, with the amount of demand at those rentals. You can complain about the prices, whether they should be higher or lower, but the supply/demand ratio is never wrong. It is what it is.

In markets where the media reports that prices are too high for the average renter, this is simply not relevant. There is enough rental demand to meet the existing supply and their prices. The successful property owner is operating a business and, as with any business, there is a fine balance between not charging enough and losing out on potential income and charging too much, which could lead to extended vacancy periods.

The sophisticated investor looks at the trends of what happened in the past to determine where the values are right now. But if more people are entering the rental market than new rentals, then the existing product will rise in value. Not every new employee will locate in the market, but enough will. More employees leads to population growth, which creates rental demand. This will lead to a rise in rental values, meaning **Increased Rents**.

It may take some time for the next step to happen. The Success Formula suggests it will take a full 18 months, with rising rents, before the next phase truly kicks in. However, eventually employed tenants will want to settle down in a neighborhood near their employer. They will want to develop roots and buy a place to live. This naturally leads to a higher **Property Purchase Demand.**

Much like current rental rates, current housing prices are based on the supply and demand of the housing market. If there are enough buyers who can buy a home, the properties will maintain their value. If more qualified buyers enter that housing market than the inventory can support, there will be upward pressure on the existing homes and values will rise. Simply put, there will be **Increased Property Prices** throughout the market with growing demand.

Let's now bring this back to how all of this information can help you build wealth. When you find a market where GDP is rising, the population is growing, and rental values are surging, you can be confident that within the next one to two years, there will be a rise in property value.

Let's use a bowling analogy. If you line up correctly and throw the ball properly in the beginning, it is logical to expect a good result in the end—you might even get a strike. In real estate, the market forces involving GDP, population, and rents are equivalent to throwing that bowling ball. If the market fundamentals are strong, it just makes sense that the property values will rise.

Continuing the bowling analogy, it doesn't matter that prior "frames" provided strong results, as none of that has any bearing on the results of this throw. In the real estate market, it doesn't matter that prices have been surging for years in the past. The economic numbers today are the equivalent of that crystal ball that you need to determine the future.

We live in a time where the information we need to make an informed decision is readily available to those willing to look for it. However, very few do that research. Become the insider in your community. Learn the markets where the fundamentals are strongest and invest in those markets. It's really hard to screw this up when you purchase your properties where tenants want to live and buyers want to buy. You don't need to spend a lot of time and money seeking out this data; it is often available for free on national, state, provincial, and local levels. In Canada, I'd start off with Stats Can (www.statcan.gc.ca). In the US it might be fun to start off looking at the US Census stats (www.census.gov/data.html). But then dig down. Maybe even contact your local town hall to see what information they have regarding future growth estimates.

"Hey Boo Boo...I'm smarter than the average bear."
— Yogi Bear

 # ARMCHAIR MINDSET PLAYBOOK

- Just because a property is cheap, does not mean it is a good deal.

- The search for a great investment property begins with finding the right market to invest in. Follow the graph in the REIN's Long Term Real Estate Success Formula.

- Becoming knowledgeable about a market, doesn't have to take years of research. Over time, you can become a market expert.

- Understanding the history of a market is interesting, but it is the ability to understand the projections of what WILL be happening that makes for a great real estate investment.

CHAPTER 4

LEVERAGING YOUR WAY TO THE TRIPLE CROWN CLUB

"Most people overestimate what they can do in one year and underestimate what they can do in ten years."
—*Bill Gates*

Try to envision a teenage Michael Dominguez. This pimple-faced kid was more confident about his future than he likely had a right to be. If you recall the character played by Michael J. Fox on the TV show Family Ties, Alex. P. Keaton was someone that I kind of strived to emulate. In fact, it was around that time that I started using my middle name initial and signing my name, Michael J. Dominguez.

As mentioned in chapter 1, by my mid-twenties I met a girl, got married, had a baby and a responsible job. My entrepreneurial spirit wasn't dead, but it was certainly on life support. It was well suppressed, as simply paying the bills, battling through a marriage, and raising an active son were the priorities at the time. I had turned into a zombie, sleepwalking through my life.

Fast forward again to my 40th birthday. Hitting that landmark birthday brought with it a realization that I had not met my goals. I had expected to be a millionaire by 35. I had expected a certain level of success by age 40. There I was in a stagnant job, recently divorced. I was starting an awesome new relationship with my eventual wife and now business and life partner, Lisa Coulter Dominguez, but I had a fraction of the wealth I thought I would have by this time in my life.

It wasn't as dramatic as me sitting down and committing to change my life there and then, but I knew the first change I had to make: I had to leave my employer. The commute, bureaucracy, in-fighting, and repetitiveness of the job was killing me. It was around that time I bought a home with my girlfriend, and it was during that process that we met Debbi Guislain. She was our Realtor, but she was also a manager of a local real estate brokerage. Traveling around with her, we discussed the industry and opportunities within it. She told me I'd make a great Realtor. I figured she said that to everyone, but she insisted that wasn't the case.

After much deliberation, I started on the journey to get my real estate license. When I was close to the end of the year-long education required to get my licence, my current employer offered me a package to leave (thank you very much). I was likely planning on leaving a few months later, but this was the push I really needed. The severance package didn't hurt either. I doubled down on my education and got my real estate license early the following year.

I began as a franchise consultant for my previous employer, and eventually became the franchise sales manager for Canada. I believed so much in the product that my parents bought a store, as did my brother. My first wife and I also bought a franchise. I really enjoyed interacting with these hard-working, business-minded people from all corners of the world. What I loved most about my role was the chance to find ways to enhance profitability at the stores.

After getting my real estate license, I quickly began to gravitate to the investors. I truly felt I was with "my people." They spoke "my language." It wasn't long before I realized the potential windfall that real estate investing offered. I didn't make my plan for the next decade right there, but I felt that real estate investing could be a big part of it.

I share my struggles and my journey so you know where I came from.

Maybe it resonates with you. It's so easy to get sidetracked along the road to success. It's far easier to do nothing than to take action. I will continue with "my story" later in the chapter.

WHERE DO I GO FROM HERE?

That is often the battle cry for so many of us across North America. We've had some success. Bought a house, built up some savings, and are moving in the right direction. However, most of us don't know how to invest our existing wealth and are afraid to take any real action because we don't want to lose what we do have. But inaction assures us that we won't meet our financial goals. It means we have to stay shackled to our jobs for the next thousand years or so.

There are a bunch of books and education seminars on various types of ways to invest and build your wealth, but I will keep it simple and put it into larger categories.

1. Equities (including stocks, bonds, mutual funds, Government Income Certificates (GICs), etc.)

2. Real estate (principal residence and rental properties)

3. Businesses (running your own business)

4. Private mortgages (lending to other people for a return)

A well-diversified portfolio of assets will comprise little bits of different investment classes. All are really good at building wealth, but don't be fooled into thinking that holding a few mutual funds makes you well diversified. Simply holding multiple equities in different sectors doesn't change the fact that they are still all equities.

In this book, I won't speak about providing private mortgages. Although it can be a solid, reliable income source for the investor, for the inexperienced and those lacking a solid team of advisors, there are a host of risks. For those with the knowledge base and the network, it can be lucrative, but it is not an entry-level investment strategy.

INVESTING IN EQUITIES

I am a big fan of the equity market. Once I learned what I could expect out of that sector, I used my knowledge built in the real estate world and applied it to equities.

I began by investing in quality, blue-chip, nationally recognized, financially sound companies, offering solid, consistent "cash-flow" dividends, in sectors I understood and that were not going anywhere. I looked for businesses that had a difficult barrier to entry, so there wasn't much threat of a competitor knocking them off. Finally, I stayed away from the get-rich-quick type of product that was highly speculative. I might have missed out on some big returns, but I was determined not to buy any of the FOMO companies and industries.

FOMO (Fear of Missing Out) is common. From the tech start-ups of the '90s to the gold rush stocks of years past to the blockchain companies and marijuana stocks in recent days, these products are in the news all the time. The general public hears about how people make tons of money in the sector and sell everything to get in. When Aunt Mary tells you that she was talking at the hairdresser and, "All the girls there decided to buy the Bitcoin," you know it's time to move on from that sector. FOMO companies only continue to rise when more "suckers" keep entering the market and buying the item. Much like a pyramid scheme, the value of the equity is not based on strong market fundamentals, but a "get-rich-quick frenzy" and it collapses when investors try to get out.

UNDERSTANDING LEVERAGING

One of the great advantages of real estate as an investment class, is the ability to "leverage" the asset. Leveraging in the investing world can be defined as using borrowed capital for an investment, expecting the profits made to be greater than the interest payable.[12]

Let me explain it this way.

You buy an asset for $100. But you don't pay the full $100 in cash. In fact, you use a percentage of your cash and borrowed money. If you were to put down $25 of your own money, and borrow the rest, then the asset would be **leveraged** in a 75/25 ratio. The reason why investors use leveraging is that they feel that the money they can earn on that asset, along with possible appreciation is going to be better than the interest needed to finance that purchase.

Lenders are almost always willing to loan you money. Depending on the asset, the leveraging percentage, your credit history, and the risk associated with it, the lender will charge an interest rate that will make them comfortable with loaning you that money.

Let's compare an equity asset with a real estate holding when evaluating risk.

EXAMPLE 1

Mr. Banker, I love your company!

I have $100,000 in cash that I wish to invest. I go to the bank of my choice. Let's say it's Bank of America, or Chase Manhattan, or maybe Royal Bank. Doesn't really matter. I go to the financial specialist, and I tell them how lucky they are that they work for such a great company. I have done my research, attended numerous investing courses, studied financial records for years, and I just love your company. I want to invest the entire $100,000 into stocks of your bank.

Then I ask the lender, what can you loan me so I can leverage my money, so I can buy even more of your bank stocks? The lender will ask if I have any real estate holdings to secure it against, but I say, "No, I am securing it against your company's bank stock."

If I'm lucky I'll receive a $100,000 "unsecured" loan at a 5–8 percent interest rate (in 2020). This means $100,000 of my money gives me working capital of $200,000, and those funds are leveraged at 50 percent. But this may only happen if I am a good customer with the lender. I may be offered even less.

EXAMPLE 2

Mr. Banker, I want to be America's Next Great Chef!

Now let's say I'm a top-notch chef and I want to start my own restaurant. Maybe the banker has been to the restaurant where I work and knows my skill set. I tell the banker that I have $100,000 to invest and want to leverage that money to buy some equipment, supplies, and inventory.

The lender will not loan on inventory or goodwill but may offer me a loan on some of the equipment. If I am fortunate, I may be able to secure a business loan of about $50,000 at a higher interest rate, because of the risk of opening up a restaurant. Regardless of how skilled I am, so many restaurants have failed and there's a lot of risk in loaning money in a business with a poor track record.

EXAMPLE 3

Mr. Banker, I want to buy an investment property!

Let's say I am a true newbie. I have never taken a real estate investing course or seminar. Hell, I haven't even watched an episode of Income Property on HGTV. I have had a job for a couple of years, make decent cash, but know nothing about being a landlord.

The lender will not really care about your lack of knowledge. They will look at the asset and because it's in the ultra-safe real estate sector, they will look at my $100,000 investment and happily loan me $400,000, so I can buy a $500,000 asset. They will give me an 80/20 leveraging mortgage at a very low interest rate.

WHY WOULD THE BANK DO THAT?

The investor/businessperson with the least experience and knowledge is "awarded" by the best leveraging opportunity at a significantly lower interest rate. Banks are not in the business of losing money. It's a safe risk for them.

Here are some interesting stats. A report issued by the Canadian Bankers Association as of January 31, 2019, looked at the number of mortgages currently in arrears across Canada. Their definition of being "in arrears" is owners being three or more months behind on their mortgage payments.

Across Canada, there were more than 4.5 million houses with mortgages and just 11,742 or 0.25 percent of homes were in arrears. Even better, in Ontario, Canada's largest province, there were over 2 million homes with mortgages and just 1,916 in arrears. That works out to LESS than 1 in 1,000. That doesn't even count the 30-plus percent of houses owned in the country without a mortgage. Not only that, but of those 1,916 homes in arrears, not all of them will end up going into power of sale/foreclosure, and if they do, the lender will retrieve some, if not all, of their investment through those proceedings.

In short, the housing market is very stable. The risk for the lender is minimal.

DON'T BE FOOLED!

Don't be fooled by equity salesman, promoting mutual funds as ultra-safe investments. I personally have had salesmen advise me to sell some of my real estate portfolio in order to have more in equities, as a means of reducing risk.

A solid, well-located, cash-flowing investment property, where the tenants pay the monthly debts, is far more risk averse than any mutual fund. Their own bank tells them that real estate holdings is significantly more secure than equities or businesses.

I like equities and I have a strong track record since I had always focused my strategy on blue-chip, dividend-paying companies. But my success record on "stock-picking" is no better than 75–80 percent, meaning at least 20 percent of the time, the company I have selected has not performed to my expectations and I have lost money as a result. The track record for savvy real estate investors is simply better.

OUR STORY—CONTINUED

We started our real estate investing journey in 2009. At the time we owned a principal family home worth about $600,000. We had little or no debt on it at that time. Ten years later that same house, with a few improvements since then, is now likely worth about $900,000. If we did nothing, our net worth through real estate would have risen along with the rising house prices in our region.

But we decided to LEVERAGE our principal home and use the available funds from the home equity line of credit (HELOC) as the down payment in purchasing investment properties. The lender provided me with a mortgage of 80 percent of the value of the home (the most allowable for any home purchased where the owner is not an occupant in Canada) and I used the HELOC from my principal residence for the remaining 20 percent. For those of you weak in math, that adds up to 100 percent. The entirety of the purchase came from borrowed money. We did not have to dig deep in our jeans to find some loose change. Nothing. Totally borrowed.

I was ready to buy! What did I buy? It may surprise you to learn that my first investment was a dilapidated six-unit building, in a secondary market, with low rents and mediocre tenant profile! I then followed that up with a legal two unit dwelling in a 'not great' neighborhood, attracting 'not great' tenants.

Why did I buy these? Up until this point, all of my real estate investing education instructed me to purchase the 'best deal' possible, finding properties that were being sold well below market value. The goal was to 'make money on the buy'. What I did not understand was that by buying these mediocre properties, in mediocre locations, I was not able to attract the kind of tenants I wanted to fill my units. Even after I renovated the units, the quality tenants still did not come, forcing me to compromise and select mediocre tenants that I would have preferred not to rent to. The result was a difficulty in collecting the rent, repeated damage done to my units, and added stress for me in the investing experience.

I quickly learned, if I was going to continue to work this strategy of owning investment real estate I needed to revise my thinking. It was then that I chose to only invest in QUALITY properties, in QUALITY neighborhoods, attracting QUALITY tenants and leading to QUALITY profits!

In a Buy and Hold real estate investing strategy, most of the investment books focus on the BUY as a wealth vehicle. They say that by buying a property well below market value you get an instant return allowing you to build your wealth. I feel the true wealth in real estate investing is in the HOLD. If you can have a passive investment that doesn't take much of your spare time, it is far easier to maintain that investment for years and decades to come.

Each year for 10 years we added at least one property (some with a joint venture partner), which I will go into later. We were able to refinance properties that had equity in them because of renovations, mortgage pay-down, or just market values rising. Always with borrowed money. In full disclosure, we did sell two of our properties in that time, as we decided they didn't fit our portfolio profile. See earlier note, the properties were not in QUALITY neighborhoods, not attracting QUALITY tenants, and not making QUALITY profits. We took our sales and used the available cash to keep growing.

Please note that EVERY ONE of our properties carried themselves, meaning that if there was a market correction, the rent numbers still made the property viable. ALL debt financing was being paid by the properties themselves, even after the properties were refinanced.

Fast forward 10 years, and the amount of equity in our properties (market value less mortgage debt) is five to seven times the value of our principal residence in 2009. There is simply no other way I know to leverage your current wealth and assets and grow your portfolio the way you can in real estate investing.

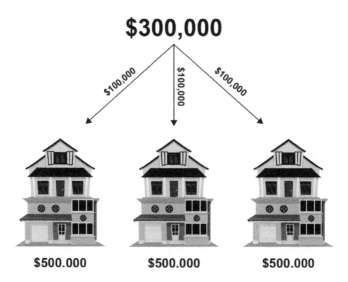

WHO WANTS TO BE A MILLIONAIRE?

Remember that game show from years past? It always seemed like the contestant was getting close, but rarely actually got there. If only there was a more surefire way to make a million dollars in your lifetime. Maybe there is!

Let's say you buy ONE investment property, at a value of $500,000. It is in a quality area, with good fundamentals, and sees a 3 percent rise in value annually for 30 years. (That is barely keeping up with inflationary rates.) Meanwhile, you bought this property with 20 percent down payment, or $100,000 in a 30-year amortized mortgage. Let's assume that in 30 years, you generated enough cash to cover the expenses, including debts, but never received one dollar in cash flow in all 30 years. Some might not even call this one a good investment. But, at the end of the 30 years the debt is all paid off and the property is worth well over $1.1 million. Even with paying back the original down payment, you are left with more than $1 million. And that is with just one property.

My goal for everyone reading this book is to figure out a way to get to three investment properties in their portfolio. This is what I refer to as the Triple Crown Club. Assuming that same growth rate and terms, the investor reaches the MILLIONAIRE rate in just 10 years.

There is no one way to get to three properties. However, there are traits that **most** of my investor clients have in common, which include:

- Having equity in their principal residence
- Getting forced appreciation by focusing on properties that need renovations
- Buying properties that can see positive cash flow after all expenses are covered
- Committing to the process, attending seminars and meet-ups and going on investor tours

I have had clients make it to the Triple Crown Club never having owned a property before, and not having much net worth and/or a reliable income. The number one thing everyone had in common was true determination to move forward and TAKE ACTION.

	Purchase Price	Down payment	Approx Balance after Year 10	Market Value
PROPERTY 1	$500,000	$100,000	$305,000	$740,000
PROPERTY 2	$525,000	$105,000	$320,000	$777,000
PROPERTY 3	$550,000	$110,000	$335,000	$814,000
	$1,575,000	$315,000	$960,000	$2,331,000

Table 1. Triple Crown Club Chart

By obtaining three properties with a combined market value of around $1.5 million, just holding on to these assets, and having the tenants pay the bills, the combination of mortgage paydown and appreciation CAN bring you a million dollars in wealth, even after paying back the original down payment amounts.

There are a bunch of disclaimers I want to address in the example given above.

- The mortgage paydown balance assumes a 30-year amortized mortgage. The calculated balance assumes interest is compounded semi-annually, not in advance. The calculations assume all payments are made when due. Calculations assume that the interest rate would remain constant over the entire amortization period, although actual interest rates may vary over this time.

- The example used a mortgage interest amount of 3.2 percent.

- We assumed an average annualized market value increase of 4 percent over the entire 10-year period.

- There was no allowance for cash flow or cash deficits over the life of the property.

- The three properties had a market value of about $500,000 each and were in a market that has suitable rent numbers to support the valuation.

Obviously, every market is different and no market sees a market value consistently rising each year—if you are in a market that doesn't see a 3–4 percent market value increase, the growth will be slowed—but this example drives home the point that you don't need to buy 10 or 20 properties, nor turn this into your full-time profession to make a real difference in your net worth. If you can find a market where the property generates positive cash flow, the numbers can look even better.

If the market you selected has prices far lower (or higher) than this example, as long as the market fundamentals are solid and the property at minimum covers its expenses and remains in a positive cash flow situation, factor in the price adjustment into the quest for $1 million in growth. A $250,000 price point would require six properties, with a 4 percent growth to achieve $1 million in equity. A $750,000 property, with the same criteria would require two.

But once you have a decent portfolio, the combination of buying the assets + time works in your favor. Time is your friend! As I have mentioned many times before, the key to being able to successfully HOLD the assets and work with the tenants starts with owning QUALITY PROPERTIES.

NOT A GET-RICH-QUICK SCHEME

Just like any industry, there are investors in the real estate sector who buy and sell quickly. These "flippers" often try to improve the property while they own it, and quickly try to turn a buck by netting more than they spent along the process. Many of these people depend on the market growing. In addition, being a flipper, done well, is a full-time job. You can't be passive or have a team to manage in your nine-to-five and still expect to be a successful flipper. That requires WAY too much effort for a guy who prefers to sit in his armchair and wait for the rent cheques to roll in.

Flipping is far too scary and speculative for me. I consider myself a **risk-averse investor**. I don't travel to Las Vegas and "bet it all on black" on the roulette wheel; in fact, when I gamble, I am only prepared to lose $100–$200 or so a day. So, why would I bet my entire wealth on some real estate or equity bets, where there is a real possibility that I could lose big time?

An excerpt from Thomas Beyer's very good book, 80 Lessons Learned: On the Road from $80,000 to $80,000,000:

"Real estate is not a get-rich-quick scheme, it's a get-rich-for-sure scheme. Real estate is predictable...boring even. However, in terms of growth of real estate and the mechanism it employs to make you wealthy, it is indeed fairly predictable. This does not mean there aren't once-in-a-generation market corrections that wipe out many real estate investors, as we saw in 2008–09. What it does mean is that generally, if you follow the rules and a well-worn path to real estate wealth, you will most likely achieve the result that so many others have, which is moderate to outstanding wealth creation."

Sounds great, but where do I get the down payment money?

One of my favorite comedians, Steve Martin, once spoke about the secret formula to becoming a millionaire. After a long setup about how HE can teach us to make a million dollars, he said, "First, get a million dollars." Yeah, it helps to have money to make money.

The single most popular way to move forward is to use equity from your principal residence and use line of credit funds in order to get that down payment cash. If you do own your own home, consider using this, or any other asset you might have to borrow against, or even sell if necessary, to get you one step closer to the Triple Crown Club.

If you are not currently a homeowner or are willing to go "all-in" with building wealth through real estate, consider moving into the unit itself. I go into way more depth on this subject in the chapter on Millennial Profit. In Canada, choosing to live in the home yourself offers you the advantage of buying that home with far less of a down payment. This strategy may not get you to three properties, however, even buying one property will bring you one giant step closer to that Triple Crown Club.

A third real option is to partner with, or get co-signer support from, another party. The "bank of Mom and Dad" might not come with ready money, but if their good credit can allow you to move forward, it might be worth the conversation. This can even be a partnership if necessary, as it will greatly benefit you, so as such, even offering them a percentage of the deal for their credit approval can be a good deal for everyone. It's fair to think that your folks might also be thinking about how to better build their wealth to secure their retirement. It's certainly important to sit down with them to discuss something that can be win-win for both parties.

Joint venturing is a proven way to move forward. The premise is that two or more individuals combine their skills and resources and work together to buy a property. I won't dive deep into the process, as there are a number of quality books focused entirely on this method.

Beginning the journey may be a little rocky. Lenders, too, can offer limitations. Most people run into these roadblocks and give up. The road may not be perfectly paved to proceed, but the few who press on and find another way to take action, who move past the barriers and get the property up and running, typically wind up winning in the end. It's only then that the process becomes a little more passive.

SELF-SUFFICIENT PROPERTIES

The temptation will be to find attractive inner-city condos, waterfront homes, and other places where you yourself would want to live. Yes, the property needs to be well-located in a great neighborhood, however, as important as all the market and property fundamentals are, the property also needs to be **self-sufficient**.

What makes real estate so wonderful when it's generating cash flow is that if something bad were to happen to me, it can be part of my safety net. Although I hope this never happens, if someone has a heart attack, gets laid off, or simply can't earn any income for the next couple of years, because they are cash-flow positive these properties will still cover their own expenses, hopefully throwing a few dollars the investors way at the same time.

Even if there is a market correction, self-sufficient properties do not need to be sold off for you to survive. The market value is irrelevant as long as the asset continues to offer you returns. The market value only really matters when you buy it, sell it, or refinance it. Positive cash flow is important all of the time.

REACH FOR THE END GOAL

The goal—the dream, in fact—is to generate enough monthly income to cover all of life's expenses. Once you reach the level where all your bills, travel, and more are supported by the revenue from your asset portfolio, you have reached a point of financial freedom. This does not mean you need to immediately quit your job, however it sure is comforting to know that your money is making you enough additional money to support you. It's like having another income-earner in the house contributing to the household expenses.

Each acquisition, each step, each connection, should be designed to bring you one step closer to reaching your ultimate goal of wealth and financial freedom.

And remember, there is a major difference between avoiding procrastination and acting irrationally. Huge, mega projects in the real estate industry, such as development deals, can be extremely lucrative, but unless you are the expert in the room, they're not much different to making that bet in Vegas.

"Money is my military, each dollar a soldier. I never send my money into battle unprepared and undefended. I send it to conquer and take currency prisoner and bring it back to me. Business is war."
—Kevin O'Leary (Shark Tank and Dragon's Den Venture Capitalist)

 ARMCHAIR MINDSET PLAYBOOK

- It doesn't matter at what age you start your journey towards building wealth, as long as you eventually do start.

- An investor can increase their return on their initial investment by leveraging the asset.

- Real estate investments in good locations have a very low failure rate by the lending institutions.

- The Triple Crown Club, of owning THREE cash flow generating investment properties locks in savings. As the tenants pay the mortgage, the principle balance goes down over time. Add in some appreciation and some monthly cash flow and you have yourself an appreciating asset.

- Real estate investing is not a "get rich scheme", but over time, it is a "get rich for sure scheme"

- Using equity from your principle residence or from the bank of mom and dad are two ways to come up with the money needed for the down payment.

🌴   True financial freedom is when you have enough residual
     income coming in from your investments to cover all of your
     living expenses, with money to spare.

CHAPTER 5

I'VE GOT THE POWER!

"The way to get started is to quit talking and begin doing."
—Walt Disney

Over the years, I have heard dozens of reasons to NOT move forward in real estate investing, but most have to do with a perceived lack of time or a lack of knowledge.

I HAVE NO TIME FOR THIS.

The ironic thing about that comment is that by dedicating time and effort into something that can build real and sustained wealth, you will actually have more time available to do the things you want to do. More money gives you more choices.

If you look at any successful person, there will have been countless times when they missed the mark, but through action and repeated action, were finally able to figure it out.

Heck, maybe they haven't yet figured it out totally, but they've figured it out enough to be successful. We've all read and heard the stories of the inventors who failed thousands of times before finally "striking gold."

Our Doors to Wealth Real Estate Group team of investor Realtors conduct investor tours at which potential clients meet us at a designated location, then carpool around with us as we discuss the areas of the community; advantages and challenges of investing; different styles of homes available; how to legalize a secondary suite; how to select and deal with tenants; a breakdown of the finances; and of course an explanation of what's required to maximize the profitability of the properties we view on that day. You see, on the tour we view five to seven properties currently available for purchase, some on the Multiple Listing Service (MLS) system, some exclusive.

Over the years, I've found that:

- If a client is unwilling to meet with me in my office, over lunch, or at one of our team's investor tours and insists on meeting me at his or her house, claiming they're too busy to meet anywhere else, that client has never gone on to take action and buy a property with us. Not once!

- For every five potential local clients who want to get on our database, just one will agree to go out on our investor tour. Very, very few have ever taken action without attending our investor tour.

- For every four attendees of our investor tour, one will end up buying a property.

- For every investor who buys one property with us, nearly all of them end up buying a second one. (Certainly at least 75 percent of them.)

Action-takers vary by age, gender, personal wealth, and heritage. There is no way to look at a person and determine that this person will be the one who takes action. That said, there are absolutely some common traits among the action-takers in our group.

- They are always networking with like-minded individuals.

- They continue to learn what is happening in the industry.

- They follow mentors who are achieving what they want to achieve and emulate those behaviors.

- They build a winning power team.

- They figure out a way to move forward by seeing obstacles and challenges as short-term speed bumps on their way to success and not a reason to stop.

Stated again, you can still do well bouncing around with whatever mortgage broker, Realtor, lawyer, accountant, or other business professional gives you the best price, but the best, and most successful, real estate investors I know, the ones who really thrive in this industry, realize that it takes a power team to maximize their success.

Build Your Team

MORTGAGE BROKER OR AGENT

We will use the example that your goal is to get to three investment properties. Most of us don't have the funds to buy three investment properties free and clear (without lender financing). A good mortgage specialist will work with you and see where you have strengths and weaknesses in your credit worthiness by primary lenders.

Depending on your situation, I recommend meeting with the mortgage broker as far ahead as six to 12 months before you are ready to actually take action.

Why so long?

Because, until you KNOW you can qualify for a mortgage with a primary lender, you are never 100 percent sure. Lenders really look for three primary things when determining a candidate's credit-worthiness.

1. Income

2. Credit score

3. Total Debt Service ratio (TDS)

But what separates a great investment mortgage broker with one you just don't want to work with?

Remember, you're trying to buy three properties, not just one. (Who knows, maybe even more.) A great mortgage broker sees the big picture in your goals and works the plan accordingly.

There are lenders who have more of an appetite for multiple-investment property portfolios than others. Sometimes a lender offers very competitive rates and a great service, but only for clients who own one or two properties. There are also lenders that offer the mortgage brokers better terms for putting a client into a mortgage with their institution. Essentially, the broker can make more money by choosing one lender over another.

A good broker will create a road map right from the start, focusing on one financial institution, then the next, and so forth. Initially, the broker may not be getting quite the same terms as with other lenders, but in the long run, more deals can be completed.

Much like staging a house before you sell it, a good broker can "massage" your numbers to get them looking their absolute best. Remember, it's not like it was 25 years ago. You don't go to the bank in your best suit and ask for a mortgage. In most cases, the branch manager has little to no authority to approve a mortgage. Your numbers are entered into a program and, based on those entries and what the algorithm comes out with, the lender determines whether or not to move forward with the loan. It's way easier for the person behind the computer screen to say NO than it is to say YES. Most lenders are salaried workers who are more interested in keeping their job than working with a borrower and understanding their file.

So, don't get mad at the game. Simply understand the rules, use people that best know how to submit the numbers to look their best, and then use them to win.

FOR EXAMPLE:

The TDS (Total Debt Service) is likely the easiest to adjust (for good or bad). By altering your monthly payments, perhaps with a consolidation loan, or just paying off some outstanding balance, it can have a significant impact on your ability to qualify.

Eliminating car payments, paying the last of your student loans, lowering your monthly mortgage payments, moving to low interest credit cards, and consolidating a number of loans with one lower monthly rate are all clever ways to lower your monthly expenditures and will have a direct impact on your ratio.

CASE STUDY
IS EVERYONE ON YOUR BOAT ROWING IN THE SAME DIRECTION?

A mediocre mortgage broker doesn't always plan ahead. One of my client's mortgage brokers convinced them to refinance their principal residence in order to pull as much out of the home as possible. The plan was to extract enough cash to use as down payments for two future investment properties.

However, the interest on the refinance was higher, the terms not as favorable, and the amortization much shorter. My client, trusting the mortgage broker, moved forward with the undesirable loan, because they felt that the wealth they could generate from the two new investment properties would more than make up for the higher interest loans.

After completing the new loan, they now had a significant amount of cash in their bank account. However, when they wanted to move forward and buy a property with a primary lender, they learned that the new loan screwed up their TDS ratios, thus making them a high risk to most lenders. Despite having a proven track record in real estate investing, a track record of making every mortgage payment, and more than enough cash to use for down payments, they were denied by every primary bank.

They later learned that the mortgage broker chose the first lender because she received higher commission fees for putting the loans together. Had the broker taken a more conservative and objective approach, the client could have received an A-rated mortgage and line of credit for their principal mortgage and been able to use the funds to buy one investment property with an A lender.

But now they had to use a B lender or even a private lender in order to close on a deal, costing them thousands of dollars. The only other alternative was to do nothing and just keep the cash in the account, while paying the high interest rate on their mortgage.

I've seen multiple mortgage brokers look at the same candidate, use the same file, but by presenting the candidate differently, a quality investor-focused mortgage broker was able to get the mortgage approval.

HOME INSPECTORS AND TRUSTED CONTRACTORS

I'm sorry to be the one to break this to you, but you are simply not the best at everything you do. The sooner you recognize that, the easier it will be to build up that team.

Many of my current clients would not believe this, but in my younger days, I renovated my first home myself, and actually built a basement rec room, bathroom, and bedroom. I learned that making the finishings look good was not my forte. I made a lot of mistakes and left behind a lot of blood, sweat, and tears in that project. To put all my readers' minds at ease, I never messed with the electrical and plumbing, but I was heavily involved in the design, framing, drywall, flooring, ceiling, painting, trim, and much, much more.

I bring this up because there are people out there with much more extensive and specialist knowledge than you. You should find these people and defer to them when you have questions.

Although I am encouraging you to take action, I'm not saying that every house will be a "home run." Some need more extensive repairs than others. Some properties look bad but need inexpensive repairs, making them a very good deal.

Years ago, I bought a property that had a caved in drywall ceiling in the bathroom, and a room in the basement apartment that had obvious water damage. My home inspector found that the foundation overall was in good shape. The house was missing a downspout in one corner and the grading went toward the house, so, naturally, water eventually made its way into the basement. But we discovered that the roof had been recently replaced, and that the main level ceiling damage came from the old roof. The damage was also localized in one area, and the damage in the attic was negligible.

The seller just wanted to get rid of her problems, and no other buyer would touch it because of the obvious water damage. As a result, I got the property for well under market value and negotiated to complete most of the repairs prior to the completion date. The property already had a legal two-unit certificate. We were able to complete the renovations quickly after the completion date and rent out the units with little downtime.

If you build your team effectively, your skill set becomes the collective of all the best people in your database.

You don't need to be the best layout designer or carpenter or plumber. If you have these people available to you, then you can benefit from their years of expertise without having to do it yourself.

INVESTOR-FOCUSED REALTOR

A police officer pulls over a car and asks the driver for her insurance and Realtor license.

The driver says, "Don't you mean my driver's license?"

The officer replies, "No, not everyone has a driver's license."

It seems that everyone knows SOMEONE with a real estate license. Whether it be a friend or family member, someone will have one. The interesting thing is that, regardless of that agent's skill set, the co-operating broker's commission will be identical. To put that in perspective, both Clayton Kershaw (star pitcher for the Los Angeles Dodgers) and I can throw a baseball. However, no one is paying me to throw that ball, whereas Kershaw is paid quite well. Yet, if Clayton and I were selling a home, assuming we both had our Realtor license, our co-operating commission would be identical, despite my years of experience.

Not all agents have the same skill set. Just because they may hold the same license does not mean they can offer the same level of service. Making the wrong decision here can set you back years, through no fault of the agent. That agent just simply didn't know any better.

In real estate, an investor specialist has thousands of hours experience specifically on this subject. Don't ask me to help you buy land or an industrial building or to lease a commercial space. The successful real estate investor has been doing this for YEARS, in many real estate cycles. It's simply not something that someone can pick up from a few weekend seminars and a couple of good books.

This quote from Bruce Lee is applicable here: "I fear not the man who has practiced 10,000 kicks once, but I fear the man who has practiced one kick 10,000 times."

A quality investment-focused Realtor currently owns investment properties. They are landlords and have built real wealth through real estate. They have dealt with crappy tenants and have been through the eviction process. They have a power team of contacts, rental leases, tons of experience, and are willing to share some of those things with you.

An investor-focused Realtor understands the municipal bylaws and won't recommend a property where you can't add a second suite. They understand the areas within the community to best allow you to attract a quality tenant. They look for added expenses in the property before you place an offer and, in some cases, work to discourage you from making bad investments.

I often joke that I am a terrible salesperson because I spend more time telling buyers to NOT move forward with a purchase or list their existing property because of certain obstacles. I want to know the buyer has enough knowledge and has seen enough properties before we make an offer. I rarely encourage a person on their first or even second investor tour to write up an offer. In some cases, investors don't want to sell their investment but are extremely frustrated over a particular situation (usually a problem tenant or an unexpected repair). Being a good Realtor sometimes means being a bit of a therapist and helping them work through their problems while offering some actionable steps to reduce their concerns.

It's important to remember why you wanted to buy in the first place. If wealth building is the goal, ask yourself if this property gets you closer to that goal. If the answer is also yes, then I would recommend finding a way to deal with the obstacle rather than just selling the property and moving on.

LAWYERS AND PARALEGALS

All real estate lawyers can close a typical transaction. In fact, with so many things available online for lawyers, including title insurance, the vast majority of real estate transactions are smooth allowing the law office to complete far more transactions in a month than ever before. You might get sucked into just shopping for price when looking for a lawyer.

Title insurance protects property buyers and mortgage lenders against defects or problems with a title when there is a change in property ownership. If a title dispute arises during a sale, or even years after possession, the title insurance company may be responsible for paying out compensation to rectify the issue.

Many lawyers use title insurance as a blanket coverage. Nonetheless, I always want to have a lawyer on my team who has been in the real estate trenches for years and can come up with a solution if a problem arises. In my experience, the vast majority of buyers and sellers go into a transaction with the best of intentions and even if issues do pop up, rational minds prevail, and a solution can be found. However, because we are dealing with such valuable assets, circumstances involving fraud, defects, legal disputes, and more can happen. Delayed or withdrawn funding, revised appraisals, deals falling through, and tenant disputes can and will happen as you build your portfolio.

We have previously sat down with members of our legal team over the years and shared challenges we've experienced. Never once did I ever stump them, where they told me they hadn't had a client who experienced a particular situation before. Whether it be a recommended course of action, right down to a properly worded clause or two, they always had a solution.

No matter how diligent you are in tenant selection, there will likely be a landlord/tenant dispute at some point that needs a resolution. While you will need the lawyer prior to the acquisition of the asset, for "minor" issues like this, you can often hire a paralegal.

A paralegal works for a lawyer, law office, corporation, governmental agency, or other entity who does legal work such as resolving tenant disputes. Although there are limits to what a paralegal can do for you, this in no way minimizes the importance of having a quality paralegal on your team.

Ideally, your paralegal focuses on representing landlords. Perhaps your paralegal also owns real estate. But the most important thing is that they have ample courtroom experience in dealing with landlord and tenant disputes. Good paralegals can also assist you in drafting your lease agreements in order to minimize any potential conflicts with tenants going forward. They understand the local landscape, meaning they know what lease policies are acceptable and ones that will be unacceptable and thrown out.

Insider Tip: Invest the time to sit in on a landlord/tenant court date. These events are typically open to the public, although rarely do people who aren't directly involved with one of the cases attend. The adjudicator may question why you are there, but when you say you are simply observing, they should leave you alone.

Sitting there for a day or two can be very educational. You will observe some of the idiotic things some landlords try to get away with, and you will see a bunch of bad tenants.

If you attend the meetings often enough, you will hear paralegals representing landlords. What better way to find a quality power team member than to see them at work representing someone else? Unlike a contractor who can show photos of the work they have completed, a paralegal can't really show you their skill set with a photo or even a well-drafted website. Seeing them in action can give you a true understanding of their skills.

ACCOUNTANT AND BOOKKEEPER

By purchasing an investment property, you are starting a small business. Just like any business, you need to track the revenue coming in and your expenses going out. Also, just like any business, you will need to pay taxes on the profits.

It may seem like a bit of an overkill to hire a top real estate accountant if your plan is to just own one property. Perhaps it is. But if it's your intention to scale the business, it makes a ton of sense to structure things the correct way. A good real estate accountant understands the tax rules and can offer you legal strategies to minimize and/or delay your tax burden going forward.

Entire books have been written on the benefits and challenges of forming a corporation for your business. I have personally attended HUNDREDS of hours of presentations that went deep into that very subject. My general answer when asked about whether to incorporate is that the investor should consult their own accountant, who can help them with this decision by looking at their specific scenario and base advice on their specific goals.

The investor needs to weigh the added costs of forming and maintaining the corporation with the short and long-term benefits. A well-designed corporation can help in minimizing potential taxes, assisting with the transfer of wealth to future generations, and reducing one's liability in the event of a lawsuit. However, owning real estate within the corporation has its limitations as well. Some lenders won't even offer mortgages to corporate-owned properties.

CASE STUDY
PAY THEM NOW OR PAY THEM LATER

Working with an accountant who understands your goals is critical. One client I worked with years ago shared with me in frustration that too much of their income generated from their rental suites was going to taxes. On one hand, they were pleased that their current portfolio was earning them profits, but the annual tax burden was actually preventing them from building enough cash reserves to add another property to their portfolio.

Intrigued, I asked them for more details. In business, you have the option to depreciate your assets while you own them. This is known as Capital Cost Allowance (CCA) and is a common maneuver used by business owners. Imagine you own a piece of equipment or an expensive tool. You use this item to make the product that you are selling to generate revenue. Over time, this item wears out and loses value. For this example, let's suggest that the tool has a 10-year lifespan. After that time, the item is nearly worthless. From a tax standpoint, it is accepted that the tool DEPRECIATED in value each year. Let's say the equipment was worth $10,000 when it was new and worth $0 after 10 years. Assuming you can depreciate the item at 10 percent a year, in year one, the depreciation of the asset of $1,000 acts as an expense to the business, and lowers the taxes you pay that year. Same goes for year two, three, etc. By year 10, the item has a book value of $0. If you ended up selling that item for $5,000, even though you had a book value of $0, you need to pay tax on the PROFITS you made from the sale of that equipment, even though it was sold for less than you originally paid for it.

Real estate assets work much in the same way. Check with your accountant first, but in many countries, you can actually depreciate the home used to generate the rental income. It is recognized that over time, the asset gets older and can lose market value. Although the depreciation rate is much slower, if you hold on to the asset for a long time, the book value can continue to drop. You likely will not be able to depreciate the land but may find that the building is depreciable.

My client had an accountant who didn't like CCA for real estate and told his clients that it would only delay the taxes, and therefore create a larger tax burden when the asset was sold.

I told my client that was absolutely true. However, what the accountant failed to grasp was that the money was far better in the investor's hands than shipped off to the government in the form of taxes. If the investor can use the extra funds to build their portfolio, and earn further profits from those added assets, it simply won't matter that they will face a larger tax burden at the time of sale.

I suggest thinking of CCA as a government-sponsored interest-free loan awarded to real estate investors. Keep in mind that these future capital gains taxes are only paid out if the asset is sold AND for a profit over the book value of that asset. If your plan is to hold on to your assets until you retire, or forever, then the benefits of delaying the payment of taxes are even better.

My client ended up finding a different accountant who would work in step with their goals. The old accountant simply would not accept that CCA was in his client's best interest.

In any business, the numbers recorded in its books is the reality of the success of that business. It tells the story of that business. Understanding how to read a company's books is so important in determining a business' profitability. It can also help you assess the business' future projections and create an estimate on the value of the business.

To most humans, the preparation of these financial records is about as exciting as watching paint dry. I have watched paint dry; I think I prefer it over the preparation of books.

However, to my delight, there are some seriously demented people living in our communities known as bookkeepers. They actually enjoy sitting in locked quarters going through and calculating a business's income, expenses, profits, and losses. The ones I have met get some sort of sick pleasure out of ensuring that everything is balanced correctly and prepared in such a way that the reader can digest the information effectively.

It is vitally important to know how to read, interpret, and make decisions based on the financial numbers of your business. This, in no way, means you need to be the one doing the task. As you build your portfolio, you should be able to compare each property against your others. If you own a number of legal two-unit dwellings, patterns should emerge with expenses. If one property has significant outlier numbers such as utilities or maintenance, it would make sense to investigate it further. If you remember your Sesame Street song, "One of These Things Is Not Like the Other," you need to investigate and find out if the problem is a one-time, short-term, or explainable anomaly, or if there's a larger issue. If hydro amounts are way higher in one unit, it may be possible that a tenant is using the premises to grow

Your power team is your formula for success.

some "plants" that are not allowed in the lease. If one water bill really stands out, perhaps there's a running toilet or slow leak in a pipe. Even if the tenants pay the utility bills, spotting a discrepancy can save you a headache later on.

Keep in mind that the beauty of building a solid portfolio, with consistent properties in comparable neighborhoods, is that the process is repeatable. You can compare insurance fees, municipal taxes, bank fees, repair bills, yard maintenance costs, and more. If your portfolio is small, don't hesitate to reach out to other investors and compare your numbers with their properties. Making some small changes to your properties can lead to repeated savings, and significantly impact your profitability and cash flow. Even if the results are minimal, it feels good to save a few bucks with a couple of procedural moves. Heck, if you study your financial portfolio and can't find a way to cut expenses or add any more income, even that should feel good, knowing that your business is operating efficiently.

MEET-UP GROUP OR BUSINESS COACH

The best athletes have a coach overseeing their performance and offering suggestions, ideas, strategies, and mindset tools to help them reach another level. Michael Jordan is a classic example of this. He was a great player early in his professional career but couldn't win the NBA championship. It wasn't until the Chicago Bulls hired Phil Jackson that the titles started piling up. During the Bulls' incredible run, Phil Jackson didn't make one assist on the court or score one basket, yet his impact was vital to the team's success.

Coaching and being part of a team, even in what is often recognized as an individual sport, is so vital in building sustained success. The same can be said about real estate investing.

The coach may never contribute one dollar toward property you buy, and the other investors may not help you qualify for a mortgage, but do not underestimate their importance. In my local market, there is an organization known as Durham REI (Real Estate Investors). Each month, the group meets. The organizer of the group is skilled at finding quality speakers, but the real power of the group is the networking before, at the break, and after the meeting.

In your friendship circle, no one is going to challenge you to push through the red tape to get that next mortgage, or head out on a Saturday afternoon and look at real estate properties. You need like-minded individuals to push and challenge you to reach your stated goals. A few years back, I had a particularly successful first half of the year and added a few properties to my portfolio. I recall my friends asking me, kind of sarcastically, "So I suppose you bought another property?" My parents worried about us taking on so much debt. There was little encouragement. Conversely, at a powerful investor group, others in the crowd applauded our success, offered ideas of how to keep moving, and kept challenging me.

How are you doing steering the boat? Are you on track to hit your goals and "finish the race?" Perhaps you're beginning to stray off course. As team captain, as important as it is to direct your team forward, in order to become a champion, you need the power of colleagues and a coach to keep you in check and help you reach your ultimate goals.

Building that power team and learning the skills takes time. But if you think about that time as an investment in reducing the amount of time you need to spend later on, it may offer you some comfort. The time spent on developing a quality power team can allow you to grow more quickly, thus reducing your need to earn income in your primary job. Drive the process, steer the boat, do the work now. Then enjoy the benefits later.

"Coming together is a beginning,
Staying together is a process,
And working together is success."
—Henry Ford

SUCCESS STORY:
Karen Jackson

Karen Jackson didn't have a traditional path to success. As she approached 40, she found herself recently divorced with two young daughters. As bad luck would have it, she also lost her job. She and her ex-husband did have a little equity in their home, but essentially no savings.

Karen was determined to make some changes. She started looking for work. Being a law clerk, there were always opportunities in that field. However, she didn't want to live "paycheck to paycheck" anymore and wanted to get further ahead, so she tried to find a way to do that. She looked into real estate and determined that this was the way she wanted to go.

She got another job as a law clerk and started reading real estate books on her lunch breaks. She felt it was a logical way to build wealth. She read books like *Rich Dad, Poor Dad* by Robert Kiyosaki, Robert Allen's *Nothing Down*, and others. Many of her family members discouraged her from pursuing this path, telling her it was too risky. But Karen pushed forward. She chose duplexes and two-unit dwellings right from the start. Her theory was that if one tenant wasn't paying the rent, she would still have money coming in.

Today, Karen's childhood friends will sometimes ask about her properties and although Karen will share stories—especially if they're positive stories, like being able to refinance and pull money out of the property tax free—the response is usually a lukewarm, "Oh yeah, that's good." They don't seem that interested. They see it as "too much of a headache" and "not worth the risk." Karen just doesn't get it. This is why she enjoys going out to networking events with other like-minded investors, because those people have a similar mindset.

At the beginning, however, her team was not investor-focused. Karen went out with her agent for almost a year to look at nearly every piece of crap on the market before she finally found a legal duplex that she wanted to move forward with. The challenge was that neither the mortgage broker nor the agent informed Karen she needed to come up with 20 percent or more for a down payment as it would not be owner-occupied. Unfortunately, she couldn't complete that deal. That was almost the end of it. She thought about abandoning this strategy, and instead, going out and looking for an additional part-time job. But, through her own research, she learned that she could access funds from her own house to use as a down payment and she later moved forward and acquired the duplex after having secured those funds.

Around that time, Karen met her life partner, Colin Newbold, and they worked together to become a forceful real estate duo. Together, they built a power team focused on real estate investing. Now that they were set up for success, once she'd got one property, Karen didn't want to stop!

They started a quest for some of the "dumpiest" properties, sometimes in questionable neighborhoods. They would renovate them completely, many times doing a lot of the renovation work and coordination themselves and with joint-venture partners. Their ultimate goal was to solely have two-unit buy-and-hold properties in their portfolio.

The duo has bought a bunch of properties and sold some too. In the early days Karen bought properties that made sense at the time, but now that her portfolio has grown, she would rather take the profits from those purchases and use them somewhere else. They now sit with about 10 buy-and-hold properties.

Karen admits that she spends about five to 10 hours a week on her current portfolio, and sometimes more when she's looking for a tenant. However, it's time well spent because the money from the properties paid for her daughters' university education. If she had stuck with the status quo, there was no way in hell she would have been able to pay for their education.

Karen was able to leave her full-time job and instead do freelance work for a law firm. In most cases, she can do the work from her home, and not have to commute into the office every day. Now she can travel without worrying about finances. She has crunched the numbers and knows she has enough money to retire.

When asked about regrets and what she would have done differently, Karen is quick to say she wishes she had known about using her principal residence for financing earlier as she might have been able to get into investing more quickly. Crucially, she would have worked with a better team from the start. Working with a Realtor team that is in real estate investing, they understand investing in properties themselves. But even more importantly, they have the right mindset and know what to look for, which is vital. If someone comes to you and says they want to buy a bunch of properties, you will be on board and encourage that person.

"The worst thing for me is that I spent over a year at the beginning oohing and ahing over many different places when I should have just taken the leap," she said. "So I would say take the leap, have confidence in yourself, and know that you can do it."

Her final advice to "newbie" investors is that it's never too late to start.

 ARMCHAIR MINDSET PLAYBOOK

- 🎯 Action takers vary by age, sex, race and personal wealth, but they are all like minded individuals in many ways and do share some common traits.

- 🎯 Building a quality power team of individuals working towards your success is a proven way to take action and create a successful real estate portfolio.

- 🎯 Improving your Total Debt Service Ratio is an important step towards qualifying for that next mortgage.

- 🎯 Not all business professionals have equal abilities. They may end up charging you similar fees, but what you can get for those fees can vary greatly.

🌴   Capital Cost Allowance (CCA) is a great way to defer taxes from real estate earnings.

🌴   If you do not have anyone in your "circle" pushing you towards your goals, find a new circle.

CHAPTER 6

THE RENOVATION DIRECTORY

"Can we build it? Yes, we can! "
—Bob the Builder

With all this talk about adding a secondary suite in an existing single-family home, you may have experienced a pang of anxiety.

You have likely wondered if adding in this suite is beyond your ability. You might have thought to yourself, There is no way I can find the time to do this work, and even if I did, I don't know nearly enough about what to do in creating that legal secondary suite.

You might very well be right. I'm certainly not going to tell everyone they have the skill and knowledge to create their own safe, legal accessory suite.

The following formula has made it easier for me to get my head around the process of making a two-unit dwelling: I think about converting a single-family home (which is essentially one big box), into two distinct dwelling units (or two smaller boxes) in the same footprint of space.

To help alleviate some of the uncertainty that comes with creating a secondary unit, it's important to understand exactly what the city and its inspectors are looking for in allowing a property owner to create that second unit. There is no magic involved.

It's important to note that codes and regulations vary by region, state, and province, and there are local bylaws that further complicate matters. On top of that, the rules are constantly evolving. I assure you that properties that were legalized 10, or even two years ago in some municipalities, may not meet the criteria today.

Think of this process as simply following a recipe. First you must understand the "ingredients" required to build that extra dwelling unit. I encourage you to check out our website, www. ArmchairRealEstateMillionaire.com for a more complete renovation directory, one that we are continually expanding. Our checklist includes photos, videos, and other links so you can truly understand how the "cake" is made. Much like making a chocolate cake, there are certain standard ingredients. Essentially, you must meet the city, town, state, or province's guidelines and regulation standards on fire, electrical, plumbing, and building in order to ensure each resident has a safe, legal dwelling space available to them. That includes minimizing the sound transference between the units and reducing the time it takes for a fire to penetrate into the unit.

I began this chapter suggesting that not everyone should attempt to do the work themselves. I have witnessed my share of "handyman specials" that have created more harm than good. Investors that want to do it the right way look at the work completed by unskilled labourers and sigh that they'll just need to rip it all out. The work completed may actually hurt the resale of the property if your eventual buyer is an investor who wants to do things the right way.

It's important to note that if you screw up a chocolate cake, the worst thing to happen is that you ruin your dessert. However, if you screw up a rental suite, you can create a fire hazard that could put your family or the residents of the dwelling units at risk. In fact, something that you have touched could have a direct role in creating a fire, developing mold, or perhaps have some other undesired outcome. People have died as a result of faulty handyman workmanship.

I don't mean to scare you off completely, but I want to reinforce the importance of learning the correct way to do things and then ensuring that your property is a safe and legal place to live.

The cool thing about the conversion/renovation process is that it has been done MANY times before. There are many courses you can take to enhance your skills. There are also many contractors available. You may not have the skill to actually finish that project yourself, but by knowing the process, you can be part of the team, quarterbacking the required work, and helping to ensure that the work is done to meet code and your high standards.

If that's even more work than you want to take on, there are general contractors out there who can work with tradespeople and help to complete the road map set out in the "recipe" for creating that legal accessory suite. But even then, I always advise my clients to know enough to oversee the general contractors. After all, you're the one paying the bill and ultimately, you're responsible if the units are faulty.

As a person taking control of your future, and trying to build wealth for you and your family's long-term welfare, it's vital that you also have a basic understanding of the ways in which developers and contractors have been building dwelling units for generations. Keep in mind, for example, that building an accessory suite (as part of an existing property) often has a different set of regulation criteria than a newly constructed purpose-built multi-unit building. The end goal is always to achieve a safe, legal dwelling unit. However, before committing to an investment, be aware that there can be some requirements in a purpose-built, new-build dwelling that can make your project unnecessarily cost-prohibitive. By understanding the local, state/provincial, and national criteria, you can save yourself a lot of time and money from contractors and inspectors who simply don't understand the rules in regard to secondary suites on existing or new-build buildings.

But let's return to our "recipe." The "ingredients" needed to build the suite will likely fall into at least one of the following categories:

1. Sound/vibration

2. Fire

3. Building/structural

However, not every "recipe" will be identical. Working with someone who has navigated through the local municipal rules is vital, as you don't want to "bake the wrong cake." That said, there are certain ingredients that are common in all cities and some of the materials will naturally have a crossover and have multiple benefits.

More than simply setting out a glossary of terms and words, hopefully this chapter will give you an understanding of what goes into the process so you can better appreciate what is required. (I will not get into the actual process or blueprint of the creation of a secondary suite here—that would be a book all on its own. Neither will I focus on local bylaws in this chapter as there are so many variations across the continent, which often have nothing to do with the actual creation of the units.) If an investor can meet the code requirement of each of the three important objectives (sound/vibration, fire, building/structural), that investor should be able to offer a safe, legal rental space; enhance their rental income; build cash flow and wealth; and get a giant step closer to their ultimate wealth goals. Let's look at the objectives.

1. SOUND/VIBRATION

Sound Transmission Class (STC) is the single-number method of rating how well wall partitions reduce sound transmission. The STC provides a standardized way to compare products such as doors, windows, drywall, and insulation. In essence, the higher the number, the better the partition is in reducing sound transference.

Below is a breakdown of STC ratings, approved by the National Research Council of Canada, and what can be heard between units based on that rating.

STC	What Can Be Heard
25	Normal speech can be understood
30	Loud speech can be understood

35	Loud speech audible but not intelligible
40	Loud speech audible as a murmur
45	Loud speech heard but not audible
50	Loud sounds faintly heard
60+	Good soundproofing, most sounds do not disturb neighboring residents

Table 2: STC Ratings

While it's true that the reduction of sound transference plays little to no role in resident safety, having a noise-free space is vital for tenants to enjoy their stay. While various provinces or states may offer different standards for a tenant's enjoyment, the reality is that the quieter a place is, the more likely it will be that you can attract and retain desirable tenants.

Remember, as property owner, you have worked hard to attract the cream of the crop tenants. You have picked the right location and renovated it to a premium tenant's standards. But once you have them in your place, the last thing you want is to lose them because one tenant is frustrated at being able to hear every conversation, nighttime activity, and bowel movement of their neighbor. If spending a little bit more attention on soundproofing during the renovation stage can make your life (and your tenant's sanity) better for the next decade or more, maybe it's worth the added expense.

So, what are some of the ways you can enhance the STC rating between units? It's impossible to provide you with a definitive list as preferences and requirements vary between areas. You can find photos and videos of some of the criteria on our website www. ArmchairRealEstateMillionaire.com as well as regular updates of when new products come available and when provinces or states create new requirements.

As always, check with your municipal office to get a better grasp on the requirements of that town or community. There is no question that their goal is to follow the state or provincial building code guidelines. However, there is often a level of interpretation that will vary town by neighboring town.

Below is a summary of the criteria most commonly employed in the process of enhancing your STC rating and a directory of materials needed to create an ADU (Additional Dwelling Unit) in an existing home.

RENOVATION DIRECTORY PART 1

Insulation. One, perhaps even two layers with a 1/2-inch gap between them, situated in the floor boards of the upper unit (or above the ceiling of the lower unit) is a great place to start enhancing your STC rating for a basement apartment. This is also the case for adjoining walls in a side-by-side two-unit property. Insulation absorbs the sound that would easily travel through the air pockets between wall framing. Major insulation manufacturers create 3½-inch thick fiberglass or rock wool batts specifically for this purpose. They are all excellent at absorbing sound. They are designed to fit in between standard floor studs, being either 14½ inches wide or 22½ inches wide. Batts can be friction-fit in wall and ceiling cavities. If temporary support is needed, consider adding in a couple of strands of drywall tape across the studs to keep the insulation in place.

More or thicker drywall. In Ontario, building code requires a minimum of 5/8-inch fire-rated type X drywall between dwelling units. However, the thicker the amount of drywall, the higher the STC rating. Adding a second layer of drywall will help further. This simply gives the surface more mass, making it less prone to vibrate and transfer sound waves.

Resilient channels. These metal strips are attached perpendicular to the floorboards, and the drywall is then attached only to the channels and not directly to the floorboards. The channels act like shock absorbers for vibration. As the person above is walking across the floor, the vibration travels down through the floorboards (attached to the upper unit floor) and then is muffled by the resilient channels, before passing by the drywall, which makes the ceiling of the lower unit.

Duct work. One of the disadvantages of a legal two-unit dwelling versus a purpose-built duplex, triplex, or multiplex, is that because the structure wasn't originally built to have separate dwelling units, there will be some allowances for some shared features. Sometimes there will be common areas inside the unit, but most often these will be in relation to utilities. Turning one house into two units requires a lot of effort. Most communities don't further require that all utilities also be separated. Duct work, by its very nature, is a system that transfers air (usually heated or cooled) from one space to another. The challenge is that you can soundproof the walls and ceilings fully, but as long as you have one duct system that connects the two units, sound and vibration will penetrate through the ducts. One solution to minimize the sound transference is to create a "sound maze" inside your ducts. The maze will still allow air to circulate through the air vent, but because of the plywood dividers and acoustic foam spaced in the duct, the sound waves will have to bounce off multiple surfaces and travel much further to get from one unit to the other, and therefore noise will be reduced.

Note that there may be requirements in your target market to use specific sealant glues, acoustical caulking, putty pads, or other devices designed to assist in muffling sound. Again, understand the STC requirements, and the local building department preferences on how best to accomplish that task.

On a day-to-day basis, it is sound transference that creates the greatest conflict between tenants in a two-unit home. A little additional effort during the renovation process and focusing on reducing that sound transference can provide you with way more "peace of mind" and "hassle-free" investing.

2. FIRE SAFETY

When it comes to general safety, it's best to not mess around. When it comes to fire safety, it's critical to ensure the safest possible unit for your future tenants so that in the event of a fire, they can escape safely and ideally without injury.

According to the National Fire Protection Association (NFPA), across the United States, "US fire departments responded to an estimated 1,318,500 total fires in 2018. These fires resulted in 3,655 civilian fire fatalities; 15,200 civilian fire injuries; and an estimated $25.6 billion in direct property loss (this figure includes $12.4 billion in losses from major California wildfires). On average, there was a civilian fire death every 2 hours and 24 minutes and a civilian fire injury every 35 minutes in 2018." According to SGI Canada, "There are about 24,000 house fires each year in Canada, resulting in an average of 377 deaths and 3,048 injuries per year."

Many times, house fires are preventable. Again, according to SGI Canada,

- The number one ignition source in all preventable house fires is cooking equipment that ignites clothing, oil, or flammable liquids;
- In fatal, preventable house fires, the number one ignition source is smoking materials, such as cigarettes;
- Fires are most likely to start in kitchens, bedrooms, and living rooms;
- In fatal, preventable house fires, more than one-third of the homes didn't have a working smoke detector.

Although it is not possible to build a home or a dwelling unit that's completely fireproof, the goal is to build a separate dwelling unit with as much fire separation as possible. In the case of a fire, the most important factor to consider is TIME: how much time will it take for a fire to penetrate through one unit and into an adjacent unit?

Again, rules and regulations for minimum standards of fire safety may vary between states and provinces. In Ontario, for example, the fire-resistance rating of the fire separation required is permitted to be less than one hour but not less than 45 minutes. The hope is that with a 45-minute rating, the occupants have ample time to be made aware of the emergency and exit the building safely.

First, let's discuss some **fire-prevention strategies** to employ in your rental units.

A) **Smoking.** Besides the obvious long-term health hazards to the participant and the secondhand smoke implications on other occupants in the house, smoking has real ramifications on the house itself. Even if a lit cigarette is never the cause of an eventual house fire, cigarette smoke and tar will penetrate into drywall, flooring, and every crevice of the home.

From a sound perspective, interconnected duct work has its disadvantages. However, from its ability to prevent in-unit smoking, duct work is your "ace in the hole." If a tenant resists the ban on in-unit smoking, the fact is that the smoke can and will work its way into the adjacent units, thus can be prohibited.

Also, as property owner, you need to enter the unit from time to time. Although you may not be allergic to smoking, you likely have a "sensitivity" towards it. Obviously, each state or province has different rules about smoking in one's private and public areas and attitudes to smoking in general.

To those who are concerned that restricting tenants from smoking inside the units will limit the number of applicants for your rental, let me share that the US Centers for Disease Control and Prevention estimates that just 14 percent of American adults, or 34.3 million people, smoked in 2017. To put that in perspective, in 1965 the figure was 42.4 percent. An even smaller proportion chooses to smoke in their residence. Across much of North America, as the building owner you have the right to prohibit occupants from smoking in the units. Use that right and set the ground rules from the start.

You should begin by presenting a ban on in-unit smoking in the lease, even posting that lovely red sign with the line crossed over the cigarette, indicating there is no smoking permitted. The goal is to simply prohibit the use of cigarettes in the units. This is your asset and the prevention of smoking in it will protect that asset. Although you likely can't restrict a smoker from renting your place, nor should you make being a non-smoker a condition of renting from you, you can and should enforce the no-smoking guidelines.

B) **Inspections.** We advocate visiting your property twice a year at the minimum. A lot can happen inside your asset and it makes me feel a whole lot better about things when we pop by and check things out. We use the excuse of the smoke detector check and battery replacement, which will be discussed later, but equally as vital is to ensure that the tenant hasn't created a spider web of extension cords through the house. An overloaded circuit is one of the primary causes of fires. Obviously, this affords you the opportunity to ensure that no exits are blocked with clutter and that there are no flammable items near furnaces, water heaters, or portable space heaters.

C) **Decommission fireplaces and woodburning appliances.** There is nothing quite like the smell of a woodburning fire. But the idea of an open flame in my rental unit just doesn't feel good. Insurance companies actively restrict the use of wood fireplaces in rental units. You may still want to have a working fireplace in your home, but whether or not the unit has been recently serviced, this is simply a risk not worth taking. If you do have a working fireplace in an existing rental, consider providing your tenant with notice, telling them that the insurance company is making you remove it. If you want to maintain the aesthetic, perhaps install a much safer gas or electric fireplace. Sorry to say, but the days of a woodburning fireplace in your rental should go up in smoke.

Insider Tip: *Should you provide a fire extinguisher in each of your rental units? The first reaction any reasonable real estate investor might* have is, *"Of course you should."* But before you go out and buy one for your units, consider these facts.

It is true that the prompt use of a home extinguisher can smother a small fire before it spreads, but fire extinguishers can be dangerous in inexperienced hands. Fighting an electrical fire with a water-based extinguisher, for example, could give you an electric shock and trying to put out a large or rapidly spreading fire with an extinguisher is useless and could leave you trapped in a burning building.

A grease fire in a kitchen can be especially dangerous. If you catch it early you may be able to put it out. But if a grease fire gets out of control, it can easily send a kitchen up in flames within three and a half minutes, leaving little time to escape.

The general consensus among fire professionals is that escaping from the home and calling 911 is the safest course of action. Most people are not trained in how to properly use a fire extinguisher and you may wind up using valuable escape time fiddling around trying to figure out how to get the thing working.

"But that's not all," as they say in the game shows. Some provinces or states, such as my market, Ontario, Canada, require the property owner to do a visual inspection of EVERY one of their fire extinguishers EVERY month. In addition, you need to have an outside company do an annual serviced inspection. If you provide the fire extinguisher and don't do the inspections, and there is a fire in the unit, the fire inspector or marshal will look to see if you've been monitoring the units correctly. The result could be some hefty fines, or charges laid against you.

This is a unique distinction between two-unit and multiunit buildings. In most apartment buildings, fire extinguishers in the common area are a requirement by the municipality and the insurance company. In two-unit dwellings, they need to be verified in your market, but because these buildings usually fall under the single-family rules, there is typically no legal REQUIREMENT. Years ago, we got a strongly worded letter from our insurance company wanting us to install fire extinguishers in each of our units. However, we pushed back, insisting it shouldn't be a requirement as there is evidence to support that a personal fire extinguisher could do more harm than good to a tenant's chances of safely exiting the building. We even told them that if they *didn't back down, we would change insurance providers. Eventually, they backed off.*

As you do your due diligence with your local municipality, verify whether it is a requirement or a recommendation before deciding to move forward with a fire extinguisher. Also, verify the requirements of the owner or your property manager on the regular monitoring of these units. This one choice could potentially add hours to your monthly obligations in your rental suites, depending on the number of units you have.

RENOVATION DIRECTORY PART 2

As mentioned earlier, some of the required items needed to complete the legal accessory dwelling unit offer multiple benefits. As such, you will see these items again.

Type X fire-rated drywall. Although regular drywall does have some naturally occurring fire resistance in its core, it is not specifically fire rated. Type X drywall, however, has special core additives that allow it to be used in fire-rated designs and it usually comes in a 5/8-inch thickness. Type X drywall will have a marking printed on the back of it, indicating it as a fire-resistance rated board.

Fire-rated doors. Fire-rated doors are used in buildings to prevent the passage of fire and smoke between two compartments or areas. Once tested, the door and frame receive a label that describes the amount of time the component is expected to provide protection when exposed to fire. When combined, all the components of the door form an assembly that protects the opening. For this reason, all components of the door must include a rating label, including the door panel, the door frame, locksets, gaskets, hinges, and door protection plates. In other cases, the entire assembly (including all hardware) has a single rating. A permanent label is attached to the door panel and the door frame, usually on the hinge side of both. Most other components have a testing agency symbol formed or stamped into the material to identify that the testing agency confirms the components meet the testing requirements.

Fireproof insulation. Nearly all insulation is rated fireproof. Most, however, only resists fire. Fiberglass batts, for example, shouldn't be used where temperatures exceed 212 °F. Mineral wool, which is recycled from iron ore blast furnace slag or made directly from natural rocks, is virtually non-combustible because of its high melting temperature and therefore excels in thermal applications. Glass wool, made from fused sand and recycled glass, traps air and blocks heat, cold, and noise. It can handle temperatures up to 1,220 °F. Lightweight, pest-proof, and flexible, wool insulation, occasionally known as "safe and sound" insulation, installs easily. A properly insulated home, with no opportunities to penetrate around the insulation, offers residents significantly more minutes to escape a fire and is often now a requirement between legal accessory dwelling units.

Sprinklers. A sprinkler system begins from a continuous water source, just like a hot water tank. To install it, we often split the water source just before it reaches the hot water tank. It has dedicated piping coming from the water source, usually copper, or occasionally plastic piping. The piping is installed in the ceilings or along the walls, often along with other plumbing. Every few feet, as required, a connector is placed in the pipe allowing the water to flow out. The sprinkler acts as a plug to prevent the water from pouring out until needed. Inside the sprinkler is a heat-sensitive trigger, usually a glass tube filled with liquid. When heat from the fire reaches a trigger, the glass will shatter, releasing the water. Unlike what you see in the movies, sprinklers not affected by the fire will not activate. It is estimated that 90 percent of fires are stopped by a single sprinkler. Although the sprinkler water will cause some damage to your unit, in comparison to the fireman's hose, it's often minimal. In some regions, sprinklers are now a requirement in furnace rooms and / or kitchens for legal accessory dwelling units.

In-duct smoke detector. In-duct smoke detectors provide early detection of smoke and products of combustion present in air moving through HVAC (heating, ventilation, and air conditioning) ducts. These devices are designed to prevent smoke recirculation in areas by the air handling systems. Fans, blowers, and complete systems may be shut down in the event of smoke detection. Often the resident of a unit will become disabled not from the actual fire, but from smoke inhalation. This device monitors the return vent, leading the air back to the furnace. If it detects smoke, it will shut down the furnace, thus preventing the smoke from circulating through the ventilation.

Without it, the furnace or A/C unit might continue to blow air through the vents, despite a raging fire in one part of the house.

Double top plate. To enhance the number of minutes it takes fire to travel between dwelling units and further increase the fire separation, some regions require all header wall joists to be doubled up at the top of a basement unit. Even though the insulation might be fire-tight, eventually the wood beam structure will lose the battle with a fire. By doubling up the 2x4 header, the fire rating between units is increased.

Interconnected fire alarms. Alerting all tenants quickly that something is wrong is vital to assuring that everyone escapes safely from a fire. However, it never ceases to amaze me how often the tenants themselves remove the batteries from their own life-saving smoke detectors because of a couple of "false alarms" coming from some burnt toast in the kitchen or something similar.

We now install interconnected, hard-wired fire alarms whenever we can, which do include a battery backup. As is required in Ontario, we verify every six months (usually when the clocks change) that the smoke detector is in operation. We often change out the battery and use that opportunity to do a visual inspection of the unit. Most importantly, we take a photo of the working smoke detector, make a record of it in our property journal, and insist the tenant signs the journal recognizing that the detector is working. In the event that a fire does happen in your unit (small or large), as the property owner you absolutely want that documented backup stating that you have been doing everything you can to assure the tenant's safety.

When a fire marshal examines the remains of a burnt home, one of the first things they do is determine if there were proper working fire alarms. If the batteries were removed or the alarm is faulty, the first person they look to blame is the property owner.

This is NOT something you can simply delegate to the tenants through a lease agreement. Imagine being in court trying to explain your position. You haven't visited your property in years. Your response is "Your Honor, I put it in the lease for the tenants to replace the batteries." I find that whenever I even remotely ponder doing "the quick fix," which may not quite be to code, I imagine that one day

I am testifying at court and whatever my explanation is, I throw the words, "Your Honor" in front of it. That tends to get me to do things the right way.

On our website www.ArmchairRealEstateMillionaire.com you can find an example of a simple chart that we use to verify that the detector and batteries have been checked. Yeah, it is simple. However, if you overcomplicate it, there's a good chance you won't use it. Simple but effective.

Strobe light fire alarm. In addition to emitting a loud sound, this fire alarm also flashes a bright light over and over again. Designed to be able to warn the hearing impaired, it will certainly get the attention of any resident in the home. Although far more expensive than the traditional fire alarm, this alarm is now required in some regions in EVERY bedroom and living room in both residences in a legal two-unit dwelling.

Fire barrier plastic pipe device. These devices are designed to fit around a plastic pipe and to be a firestop through the piping for up to two hours. They come in various sizes to fit different sized piping. There really is minimal assembly required on these things. In the event of a fire, the heat and flames make their way from one area to another. One such area with little resistance is the water pipes. If you think about it, the piping carries through the entire home, and a fire can penetrate through the fire barrier quickly in this way. As the plastic piping melts from the heat, the barrier acts as a clamp, preventing the fire from passing through.

There is no way to be able to assemble a complete list in this directory, as things are always advancing and new products always coming out. I have, for example, left off some smaller fire-safe items, such as sealant, strips, tape, putty, and likely more. Every region across North America has their own spin on things. All are focused on resident safety.

Insider Tip: when a building or system is said to have a "one-hour fire rating," that indicates that some of the construction elements and/ or assemblies in that building have met and satisfied the relevant standard fire resistance test.

There is always a fine balance between cost versus safety and comfort. If there were no budget limit whatsoever, we could build a fireproof, soundproof fortress in every unit. However, in reality this balance does need to exist. You should strive to meet minimum code at the very least. The local building department will give you a template to follow to meet or exceed the state or provincial building code requirements.

In our personal experience, we have been blessed not to have had a house fire in any of our properties. Long may that continue.

3. BUILDING/STRUCTURAL

The final component of the directory deals with items directly related to building code. Again, this varies greatly by region and we recommend that before you begin any project, you verify with your local building department to see what requirements you must comply with.

The main purpose of building codes is to protect public health, safety and general welfare as they relate to the construction and occupancy of buildings and structures. As a realtor, I have seen far too often home owners and unlicensed contractors complete shoddy workmanship that is simply unsafe for the home's residence. Below is a breakdown of some of the areas of focus that building inspectors review in determining the safety and comfort of the future home's occupants.

RENOVATION DIRECTORY PART 3

Natural light (windows). Often, accessory apartments in basements, attics, or above garages face a challenge of not having enough natural light. Besides the obvious rentability concern of a residence with few or no windows, many regions stipulate minimum standards of the amount of natural light per room in order to allow for a legal secondary suite.

In Ontario, they measure natural light per room by comparing it to the size of the room. For example, if a bedroom is 100 square feet, the minimum requirement of natural light in that bedroom is 2.5 percent. This means that the length x width of the window glass must be at or greater than 2.5 square feet (2.5 percent of 100 square feet).

If the bedroom is 150 square feet, the window glass must be at least 3.75 square feet. The natural light requirement for living rooms is 5 percent. Kitchens and bathrooms have no minimum light requirement. Depending on your apartment design, it may be possible to use the exit door window to achieve your minimum light requirement. Some designers actually replace their front door with one with a much larger glass component in order to meet the regional requirement.

Egress window. The word "egress" means the action of going out of or leaving a place. Depending on your regional requirements, you may need to provide your tenant with a safe second means of escape in the event of emergency. Egress windows offer openings large enough to allow most people to get out of the unit if needed. Some regions insist that the egress window cannot be more than 3 to 4 feet off of the ground, because if it is too high up it may be impossible to access during that emergency, although a permanent ladder structure or table may allow you to have that egress window a little higher. Keep in mind that often, in a basement, the size required to create that egress window will not be sufficient to meet the standard. This means that the contractor needs to build an exterior window well, along with proper drainage, in order to achieve the required opening. It is worth noting that if the window well is massive and too deep for an average person to climb out of, consider installing a ladder or window wells with grooves in the metal in order to fit your feet into them, so you can climb out.

There are many different types of egress-sized windows available. It's important to use one in which the window can be opened easily, with no special skill or tools required. A true egress window will never be made of two panes of glass, where you need to remove the glass from the groove and practically need an engineering degree to figure it out. One lever, lift, and remove. You will want the square footage of the opening to be a MINIMUM of 3.8 square feet, with both the length and the width being at least 15 inches long (some regional requirements may vary). Plus, this is one instance where you can safely say that bigger is better.

Insider Tip: one upside to inserting an egress window is that it will create a ton of natural light in the room it's installed in. We typically try

> to install it in a living room to meet the minimum light requirements
> in that typically larger room. Also, the living room is where tenants
> often spend the bulk of their time when not sleeping. Having a larger
> window and increased natural light enhances the residents' living
> experience and often makes the unit more rentable. Finally, having
> the egress window in a communal room, versus in one of the bedrooms
> (in a two-plus bedroom home) ensures that everyone will have access
> to the exit.

Common areas. A common area is a portion of the building where residents from multiple units have access to that space. We strive to attract the highest level of occupant possible. Adding in-unit laundry, for example, is often one component that attracts premium tenants. However, there may be times, because of layout, where shared space in the unit may be necessary. That could be a hallway, stairs, an exit, storage space, or the laundry area.

The first requirement is that any shared space must be free of clutter, allowing easy access to and through that space. The common area may have increased fire code requirements. Speak to your municipal building department for details there.

If you can design your space to not include common areas, the cost in some instances may even be lower. You can avoid expensive fire-rated doors and other such materials, while offering your tenant the advantage of less interaction with their neighboring tenant. I am a big believer of the expression that "good fences make great neighbors." In this instance, the less the need to interact with your house co-tenant, the less the chance of conflict.

Carbon monoxide (CO) detectors. CO detectors are an essential requirement in any dwelling unit. They sound an alarm when they sense a certain amount of carbon monoxide in the air over time. Unlike smoke, CO is hard to detect, as the gas is often colorless, odorless, and tasteless. We have had times when the CO detector has gone off in our units. Thankfully, in each case to date it has been a false alarm. We instruct our tenants to immediately call 911 and exit the premises if the alarm goes off. We want the experts to assure us that it is safe to re-enter the building. Carbon monoxide typically is the result of malfunctioning fuel-burning appliances, such as a gas furnace, water heater, oven, or fireplace. When fuel is burned, it emits CO as a by-product.

Experts feel that at minimum you should have a CO detector on each level of the home. Positioning the detector outside of the bedrooms is often the recommended location. There are now combination smoke/CO detectors available to buy. They cost a little more, but then there is only one detector to purchase. Of course, if one component of the detector breaks down, the whole unit must be replaced.

Minimum and maximum allowable space in an accessory unit (including room sizes). It seems that nearly every region and every municipality has its own requirement for minimum or maximum space. Local bylaws often play a role in this decision. Resident safety has little to do with these requirements. While it is true that minimum sizes often are more flexible in larger cities where occupancy is such a concern, even that is not always the case. Occasionally, long-term homeowners want to limit the size of the apartment to discourage large families from locating next door.

Before selecting a market in which to begin your real estate investing business, it is essential to know if there are any local or regional restrictions that prevent you from maximizing the property's (and your) potential. Some local markets are so restrictive that the safest decision may simply be to choose an alternative market to invest in. I go into far more detail on this subject in Chapter 13, The Missing Middle.

Ceiling height. Some regional building codes provide minimum standards for a ceiling height in a legal accessory unit. This measurement is taken from finished ceiling to finished floor. In Ontario, the requirement for a basement dwelling unit is 1.95 meters (6 feet, 4¾ inches) in height over the entire required floor area, including the route inside the unit leading to the exit. This often presents some challenges when navigating your space, with existing ductwork and main-level floor beams overhead your basement apartment. By using recessed floor beams and thinner duct work, you can sometimes achieve the required ceiling height. But sometimes the only alternative is to do a basement underpinning or benching to give you the required height.

This is a complicated and expensive process that requires professionals. When simpler height-gaining solutions are not enough to legalize the property, my advice is to move on.

Electrical requirements. Often the load needed for one family differs from the load of converting the same home into two dwelling units. There will now be two fridges, stoves, dishwashers, microwaves, televisions, and so on. Some building codes require each dwelling unit to have 100-amp service. If the home shares one electrical panel, the minimum requirement, depending on the region, is likely a 200-amp panel. If you're lucky, there will already be the minimum service to the house and the electric meter. In that case, the electrician simply needs to run the higher amps into the house from the exterior of the home and not all the way from the road or even further, which would be difficult and expensive. If the home you are considering doesn't meet the required standards, my advice is to reconsider the purchase.

Septic system requirements. Simply put, two families typically use the septic system more than one family. Two families bathing and taking showers. Two families using the toilets. If your desired property has a town sewer system, it is PROBABLE that the system can handle the increased "load." However, if it has a septic tank system, you may need to install an additional holding tank to meet the increased usage and factor in the added expense.

Plumbing requirements. To legalize your second unit at minimum you will need a hot- and cold-water supply; a bathroom sink, shower and/or tub, and toilet; and a kitchen sink. In addition, second units must have their own separate water shut-off valves.

When a house is constructed, unless it's a custom-built luxury home, expect the contractor to just meet minimum code in order to control costs and make a profit in the home sale. One such example of that is in the plumbing. Often, the piping from the main water source to the hot water tank is ½-inch piping. Some regions and municipalities require the homeowner to increase the potential water flow to the hot water tank (and possibly sprinklers) to ¾-inch or larger. From a tenant enjoyment standpoint, this offers some advantages as multiple people using the water source simultaneously will impact the flow of water at the best of times. If the piping is too small or corroded, it will be like trying to get water through a hose when there's a kink in it.

> *Insider Tip:* You could consider converting your hot water tank to the tankless variety. Your tenants most likely all have jobs. People with jobs often shower in the morning all around the same time. It can be frustrating if your shower is often just cold water or becomes scalding hot when someone in the other unit flushes the toilet. Tankless heaters help to provide a continuous flow of regulated water and can make the difference for some people in whether they want to stay in the apartment or move on to someplace else.

Parking requirements. In most municipalities across North America, local bylaws require there to be at least one parking spot dedicated to each dwelling unit. This may include a parking spot in a garage or carport. They could either be side-by-side with each car able to pull out of the driveway without affecting the other vehicle, or tandem, which means one car is parked behind the other. Some local bylaws set the requirement, but sometimes the homeowner can decide.

If afforded the choice, the temptation is to save costs and just have the one parking lane for both tenants. However, imagine the inconvenience of being woken up at 7 a.m. to move your car so your partner can go to work. Now imagine if you had to wake up your neighboring tenant to jockey the cars and let you out. How many times could this lead to the other tenant "not hearing the doorbell" and refusing to move their car? The added cost of another driveway lane can help attract and keep quality tenants in your units.

There is a growing trend in larger cities to allow additional dwelling units to be legalized even if there is no parking spot afforded to it. In some cities, the public transit is spectacular, and the tenant simply has little need to own a car and incur that extra expense. The irony is that in some cities, there is a housing shortage crisis, and homeowners are restricted from creating ADUs because of a lack of space to include (required) parking spots. Meanwhile, the tenant who would likely rent the unit doesn't even own a car.

If you decide to purchase a property with the intention of creating a second suite, I recommend hiring a professional architect to create and design the plans for that added legal unit. It is much easier to get a building permit from the building department if you have professional plans. To legalize your dwelling unit, you need to be working in-step with the building inspectors.

It has been my experience that if you truly try to build the unit the right way, the building planners will want to work with you. Everyone is in agreement that we want and need safe, legal dwelling units. There may be some "unnecessary" push back and requests by the department that exceed code, but ultimately, by working together, you will achieve your goal of a quality rental unit, which will attract those quality tenants.

"Have a plan. Follow the plan and you will be surprised how successful you can be. Most people don't have a plan. That's why it's easy to beat most folks."
—Bear Bryant

 # ARMCHAIR MINDSET PLAYBOOK

- 🛈 If you don't have the skillset to do the required renovations, bring in people who can. People's lives are at risk if you provide them with substandard living arrangements.

- 🛈 Sound Transmission Class (STC) is the single number method of rating how well wall partitions reduce sound transmission.

- 🛈 Although is it not possible to build a home or dwelling unit that's completely fire-proof, the goal is to build a separate dwelling unit with as much fire separation as possible. A 45 minute rating should allow the occupants ample time to exit the building safely.

- 🛈 An egress window is one where a resident can exit from. Besides the obvious safety advantages, an egress window, being somewhat larger, also offers the added benefit of additional natural light.

As property owner, you, or a representative, should be walking through each unit to ensure the CO and smoke detectors remain installed, batteries are changed, furnace filters are replaced, and there are no unexpected surprises in the unit.

CHAPTER 7

DON'T LET YOUR INVESTMENT GO UNDERWATER

"Nothing is softer or more flexible than water, yet nothing can resist it."
—*Lao Tzu*

Flooding has become the number-one claim by insurance companies for residential homes.[13, 14, 15] It has long since surpassed damage by fire as a "loss leader" for insurance companies, which has led to insurers actively making plans to minimize the losses from flooding and water backups.

In the news over the past few years, we have seen cities around the world dealing with extreme flooding. Cities such as Venice[16] and New Orleans[17] are two of the most famous. I am not a scientist, and I don't even want to get started on the global warming discussion, but as investors we need to be aware of the new world reality and adjust accordingly.

There is a term in the environmental world known as a 100-year flood. Simply put, a 100-year flood is an event that has about a 1 in 100 (or 1 percent) probability of happening. It's generally thought to be a once-in-a-lifetime occurrence. From a flood plain and insurance standpoint, these areas are thought to be of low risk and safe from disaster.

The problem is that these 100-year floods are happening more often.[18] Towns and cities across Eastern Canada, for example, are dealing with unprecedented flooding. As the snow and ice melts each spring, rivers, lakes, and ravines rise and water works its way into streets and properties—and into basements—across the country. Some towns have now had three or more "100-year floods" in the past 20 years.[19]

In the town of Gatineau, Quebec, the province has offered each homeowner in the most severely affected areas of flood plains $200,000 to move to another location.[20] Many residents are resisting this offer, claiming that their home is worth far more than that amount. But in reality, their home is essentially worthless. No one would consider buying it from them, knowing that the property is right in the middle of an active flood plain. In addition, insurance companies simply won't cover any further damage that might one day affect the property as a result of water or moisture damage.

In southern Florida, according to revised map projections, much of that area is now susceptible to rising sea waters. "Waterfront land" in Florida may sound great but with rising sea levels, this can present a real issue. According to SeaLevelRise.Org,

> *"The sea level around Florida is up to 8 inches higher than it was in 1950. This increase is mostly due to ice melting into the ocean and, complicated by the porous limestone that the state sits on, is causing major issues. Many traditional methods of solving sea level rise and flooding in Florida won't work, because water can flow through the porous ground, up from below, and under sea walls. In Miami-Dade County, the groundwater levels in some places are not high enough relative to the rising sea levels, which has allowed saltwater to intrude into the drinking water and compromised sewage plants. There are already 120,000 properties at risk from frequent tidal flooding in Florida. The state is planning over $4 billion in sea level rise solutions, which include protecting sewage systems, raising roads, stormwater improvements, and seawalls."[21]*

Of even greater concern, they go on to say, is that its speed of rise has accelerated over the last 10 years; sea levels are now rising by one inch every three years. Being in Florida, one must also take into account the occasional hurricane that passes through. One Category 3 or higher hurricane can lead to devastating flooding. As the water levels continue to rise, these disasters are becoming more and more frequent even with a typical tropical storm.

We all know about the effects Hurricane Katrina had on the city of New Orleans. In August 2005 the storm caused the levees to fail, releasing tens of BILLIONS of gallons of water into the city. It's estimated that over 200,000 homes were damaged or destroyed and more than 800,000 citizens were displaced from their homes. Some parts of the city were simply beyond repair and remain boarded up to this day.[22]

I had the opportunity to attend the 2019 Berkshire Hathaway Annual event in Omaha, Nebraska, where Warren Buffett spoke to the crowd and answered an assortment of questions on a wide range of subject matters.

Mr. Buffett mentioned that the Katrina disaster put a number of insurance companies close to bankruptcy. Insurance companies are great at collecting payments and will cover damages in individual or regional cases, but he points out that if there were ever a natural disaster that covered a large portion of the country, very few insurance companies are in a position to cover the number of claims that could arise in that Armageddon-type event.

Counting on your insurance company, therefore, may not be the wisest course of action—even if you're not in a flood plain and have full coverage.

Obviously, you can't plan for every possible scenario before deciding to invest. But you can minimize your risk by avoiding known concerns such as choosing to avoid flood plains.

In much of North America, neither the seller nor the selling Realtor needs to disclose that the property they are selling is located on, or near, a flood plain. However, I believe it's safe to assume that if you were offered two comparable homes, and you learned that one was situated on a flood plain, you would likely purchase the home NOT on the flood plain.

It's only a matter of time before the need to disclose previous floods and proximity to a flood plain becomes as standard as disclosing asbestos or old, faulty wiring. The overall impact for those who own properties in the flood plain will be a sizable decrease in their property value, as fewer buyers will want to take on the added risk.

Many cities and towns are now restricting how homes situated on a flood plain can be used. One of the banned uses is creating a secondary suite for a separate dwelling unit. If you own that property, yes you can continue living there and using the basement for your personal space, but you simply won't be permitted to create that basement apartment. It obviously makes sense to restrict dwelling units under grade (i.e., below ground level) in flood plains. The challenge is to know where that flood plain is in your desired investment market and make sure to avoid that area.

The great news is that you or your Realtor can contact your municipality or local conservation authority before submitting an offer. Some municipalities and counties have flood plain maps that you can purchase or access online. A little due diligence prior to the purchase of an investment can save you a heap of trouble later on.

Remember, there are a lot of investment opportunities out there. Way more than you have the funds to buy. If your research finds that your target property is close to or within a flood plain, consider it a flashing emergency siren blasting at you to stay away.

It's the perfect storm of concerns. Population increases have led to urban sprawl across many towns. What was once field and dirt, allowing for better drainage, is now streets, houses, and concrete. "Ravine lots" have been in incredible demand for generations. Picturesque and tranquil, with no neighbors living behind or beside you may sound appealing, but many such homes are simply located perilously close to water. Also, there is little doubt that the overall water levels are higher today than they were a generation or two ago. Perhaps when that 1960s bungalow was built the builder didn't even consider the possibility of extreme flooding in that area.

Finally, as a means of densifying our community and maximizing the value of a potential property, often the investor needs to utilize the basement space in order to create that additional dwelling unit. Many of these basements were not initially designed to have people living in them. While I remain a huge advocate of utilizing the space and maximizing your returns, there must be a word of warning to pay close attention to water prevention in your investment.

I am guilty of not doing this. In one particular situation (see the case study below), I spent more than $100,000 on a renovation, yet resisted spending just a little more to prevent water from destroying my work and ruining my investment.

So, how can you minimize your risk to water damage?

The first thing I would advise any client to do is to take a look at your existing properties. Whether it be your principal residence, cottage, or investment property, check out how close each is located to the revised flood plains. I know of some investors who now own properties on, or near the edge of the plain. In some cases, the city allowed the use of a legal basement apartment years ago when the landscape was different.

If I owned a property on a flood plain, I would evaluate how much I really like that property. If the disclosure of flood plains becomes mandatory in any real estate sale, would I still want this property, even though the market value of it may have dropped by 20 percent or more? Would I still want to own it if the insurance company sent me a letter informing me that because of its location, the property is no longer eligible for water damage coverage (even if the property has never had a water damage claim)?

Insurance companies are actively looking at zip code and postal codes across the continent and altering coverage accordingly to reduce their risk. If you are in the danger zone it's a matter of "when" not "if" your coverage will be altered.

I always recommend to my clients that they analyze their portfolio annually to determine if they would still buy that property today if they had the chance. Most often the answer is yes or maybe even, "Hell, yes." But occasionally, because of persistent tenant issues, lack of cash flow, a decision to focus on a different geographic location, or the inability to refinance the property, for example, it actually makes more sense to grow their business by divesting themselves of some of their portfolio.

Now, let's add "proximity to a flood plain" to the list of reasons to consider selling that property. I stress that no one has the financial wherewithal to buy everything they see. This means as a property investor, the decision is between one property versus another. It's a bit like playing the game hot potato (where the participants pass around an object such as a set of keys, a beanbag, or perhaps even a potato, and continue to pass it around while the music is playing. The person holding the object when the music stops loses).

In real estate, think of the flood plain property as the hot potato. You pass along the property to the next person now, because eventually the "music will stop," in other words, there will likely one day be a major flood, insurance policy changes, or simply a need to disclose this in the sale of the property. The person who owns the property at that time will have that hot potato—and loses the "game."

If you're trying to build your portfolio, when it comes to buying a property with flood plain implications, I recommend you follow the advice of Nancy Reagan and, "Just Say No!"

I should point out that water prevention is rarely, if ever, a requirement of LEGALIZING a second suite in a property. As discussed in the renovation directory, the focus is primarily building, fire, sound, plumbing, and electrical in nature. Any money you spend on water prevention will be in addition to all the essential renovations required. As such, it's very easy to dismiss it as an unnecessary expense and choose not to do it. If you're flipping a property, (i.e., selling it shortly after the renovation is complete), the buyer will think of these added touches as nice bonus items, but rarely will be willing to shell out additional dollars for the purchase. If your plan is to refinance the building, don't expect the appraiser to raise the final appraisal value simply because of work done for water prevention.

So why do the added work?

We are buy-and-hold investors. These assets are valuable. If we can do anything to prevent disaster from happening, we should, at a minimum, consider it.

Here are some of the prevention and protection options available to homeowners and investors.

Foundation wrap. A means of waterproofing the foundation walls. The process is messy, but relatively simple in nature. You begin by digging a giant trench all around the exterior of the building. In most cases, the trench needs to go all the way down to the footings. Certainly 8–10 ft down is not unusual. After the space is opened up, a plastic membrane is applied and "wrapped" across the foundation walls. It acts as an outstanding waterproof barrier, and if properly applied simply prevents water from passing through the ground or surface and penetrating the basement. The wrap is often combined with a weeping tile or drainpipe system that catches the water along the perimeter of the property and diverts it away.

French drain. A "ditch" in the ground, inset with a perforated pipe under a layer of gravel. The pipe diverts storm water away from where you don't want it and deposits it in a more desirable space, such as a storm drain or a rain barrel. Ground water sitting along your foundation will eventually seep into the soil. The concern is that as the water seeps lower, some of it may find a way into a small crack in the foundation and work its way into the basement, causing extensive damage. Rerouting that flow of water with a French drain would alleviate that problem.

Eavestroughs, gutters, and downspouts. Often overlooked, but vitally important, these items effectively divert rainwater and melted ice from your roof and away from your building. Water always finds the easiest path of movement. If the eaves have cracks, have pulled away from the home, or are blocked by debris, the water will seep along the exterior of the building, and work its way to the foundation ground, or worse, it may find its way into the building through a window or crack. Those who have winter storms may have seen huge icicles hanging from the rooftop. Although they may be pretty to look at, they are an obvious sign that water has built up in one area and is working its way down. Ensuring that your system is free from damage and kept clean of debris is the first step to mitigate this problem and should be done once or twice a year. If you have a tree that drops leaves and branches near your property, it's imperative that you have that debris removed prior to the winter months. You need the water to work its way through the eaves into the downspout and finally ensure that the downspout diverts the water at least six feet away from the foundation and doesn't return to the foundation base. Other "debris" such as bird and rodent nests can also cause water to dam up. Certainly, eavestroughs covers are an effective but expensive solution, but just climbing the ladder each fall to ensure they are good for the winter season is equally good.

Grading the yard. Sometimes the simplest solution can be the most effective. Yet it's nearly never done effectively. In speaking with home inspectors, many of them estimate that easily nine out of every 10 homes could use at least some regrading, which means sloping the soil away from the house in all directions dropping about two or three inches for every 10 ft. The objective is not to build your house on a hill, but to create a gradual slope away from the foundation that allows the ground water to not settle adjacent to the home. This is a fairly inexpensive solution. Soil is delivered to your home and you then distribute it all along the exterior of the building packing it down, allowing for that slight slope away from the house. If necessary, then lay grass seed or sod to finish the job.

Billy is grading the house

CASE STUDY
THE $7,000 MISTAKE

I can raise my hand as guilty of neglecting water and moisture in my rental buildings, especially when I started out in real estate investing. In one case, I had purchased a property that needed a major renovation to the basement. I was determined to make this property show well so installed ceramic flooring in the kitchen and bath and high-grade laminate throughout the rest of the unit. I upgraded plumbing and electric and installed laundry, a new bathroom, and more. I did notice that the grading was poor on the property, and in fact my home inspector pointed that out prior to me having purchased the property. But I was focused on getting the units ready and collecting rent. The outside maintenance would have to wait.

Sure enough, the apartment was finished nearly on time and just slightly over budget. Because it showed so well, and was well *located, it was easy to rent. Just weeks after the tenant moved in, who had a new baby, I might add, she called to inform me that she was seeing mold forming in the kitchen cabinets and along one wall. I quickly learned that the rain had settled adjacent to the foundation, and because of the poor grading, had worked its way into the unit. I quickly sprang into action. The tenant moved in with her parents for the rest of the month and we ripped out the damaged kitchen cabinets. We replaced the wet drywall and improved the grading on the exterior of the building. Had I added the dirt at the beginning, the repair would have been under $1,000; however, with the lost rent, new kitchen cabinets, and other small repairs the total cost to me was actually $7,000. I think of this like an expensive university course I would like to not take again.*

Interior French drain. Sometimes it's far easier to "catch" the water seeping through the foundation from the inside of the property, rather than building that exterior barrier. In these "wet" basements, water presses against the foundation and eventually leaks through. With an interior French drain, the water can be caught at the foundation and diverted somewhere else. Much like the exterior French drain, the trench is created by cutting into the basement floor and installing the drainpipe and gravel. Once the water seeps into the pipe, it's diverted to a central location, often with a sump pump, which directs the water from the interior of the house to the exterior.

Sump pump. A submersible pump is used to remove water that has accumulated in a water basin located below the basement floor. When water builds up in the basin, the pump kicks in and transfers the water to the desired location outside. Some homes need a sump pump more than others, but take it from personal experience: it's vital that when the pump is needed to kick in, it actually does what it is supposed to do.

CASE STUDY
CANDID CAMERA

We neglected a seldom-used sump pump and, sure enough, when it was needed, the pump had seized up and didn't work.

Consequently, the water rose to beyond the basin lip and worked its way onto the floor of a vacant unit we had. Thankfully, we found out about the problem before the water had spread beyond the kitchen and hallway area. Amazingly, my wife Lisa went to the property on the day of the back up to shoot a video of the vacant unit. We still have an outtake of Lisa starting the video, talking about the features of the area, and describing the unit as she walks down the stairs. When she reaches the bottom she pauses for a moment, then quietly says, "Ahhh," and shuts off the video. It could have been a total disaster of our renovated unit but we got lucky. A working sump pump would have solved that.

Flood detection sensors. Maybe it's time to consider a more high-tech solution to navigating through the water issue. These devices won't prevent moisture and water from entering your property, but what they will do is let you know quickly that something is wrong. Having a water leak sensor and wireless flood detector with instant notifications and by-the-minute water use data sent right to your smartphone can allow you to identify a problem before it becomes a real disaster. Typically, there is an upfront cost to each of these units, and most companies charge a monthly or annual monitoring charge. However, some insurance companies offer reduced insurance premiums, which can help to offset some of those expenses.

CASE STUDY
WARNING...WARNING

Last year we received an alert that one of our properties had a warning-level amount of water usage. This was a property at which we had had a leak before (see the sump pump story). We called the tenants to see if there was anything obviously wrong. The lower level tenant said she saw no water seeping from anywhere and that everything was fine from her end. However, the upper level tenant wasn't answering our calls or texts. The tenant is an older man with failing health. The lower tenant could hear the slight sound of water running in the bathroom area (the bathrooms are directly above each other). After a series of missed calls, Lisa was increasingly concerned. She feared that the tenant had perhaps fallen in the bathtub and might be injured or worse. So we headed to the property and saw the tenant through the window lying on the couch. We knocked on the door repeatedly and with more and more force, until finally he slowly stirred and came to the door. After a series of apologies, we explained why we were concerned and he told us that he hadn't been feeling well and took some medication that knocked him out. He let us in and we quickly discovered that the toilet had been running for the past five to six hours! We did a temporary fix, and eventually replaced it for him. In this case, everything worked out well, and the tenant was grateful that we were so concerned for his well-being. Had the issue been a leaky water pipe, or an overflowing toilet or bathtub, the situation could have been far worse and much more costly to repair. This turned out to be a false alarm, but it proved to us the importance of knowing when something unusual is happening in our investment assets.

Mold-resistant paint. Mold-resistant paint does typically cost more than traditional paint, but keep in mind that all basements have higher levels of moisture because they are subgrade. Where moisture levels are higher, paint is more likely to peel, and surface mold can build up. Although often overlooked, using specialist mold-resistant paint can prevent unnecessary repairs further down the line.

Exhaust fans and humidity sensors. Not every region requires an exhaust fan in bathrooms in order to create a legal accessory apartment. Regardless, it's a smart addition to any new apartment. Even if there is a bathroom window, the reality is the window often remains closed and the humidity stays in the room and the apartment. We try to take it one step further by combining the exhaust fan on the same switch as the light. As long as the light is on, the fan will also be on. The only problem with that is that as soon as the shower is finished and the tenant leaves the room, they turn off the light and the fan shuts off despite the high humidity levels still in the room. You can ask the tenants to remember to leave the fan on for a few minutes after the shower, but there is little guarantee that this strategy will be effective. We now try to install a humidity sensor in the apartment bathrooms, so when the humidity hits a certain level, the fan turns on, even if the bathroom light is off.

Attic hatch door insulation. To those who remember their high school science lessons, we know that heat rises. My home inspector has been telling me for years about the importance of insulating the attic hatch door. When heat rises, the warm air can find its way through the hatch door and into the attic. Simple weather stripping along with an added layer of insulation on the back of the door can greatly reduce heat loss. Besides a higher heating bill, the greater concern is that when the warm air meets up with the cold roof on a winter's day, condensation builds inside the attic. Over time, the attic wood will develop "sheathing" which is basically a layer of mold. If left untreated, the mold spores can work their way into the rest of the house, potentially causing a whole host of health issues. Once the hatch is insulated, and the warm air is no longer working its way into the attic, the spores will dry up and the threat is greatly reduced. However, if the problem is severe enough, the wood will have to be removed, which will likely entail removing and replacing the entire roof shingle. There are ways to clean the sheathing without having to remove it, but that often requires a professional. Lowering humidity levels in the home, eliminating all leaks into the attic, and ensuring there is proper ventilation allowing heat to escape from the attic are all important factors to consider.

Dehumidifier for window condensation. Condensation is the result of relatively warmer and more humid air meeting a cold surface. If left untreated, this can be far more than a minor annoyance. Water can build on the window frame, leak down to the drywall or plaster below, and create mold and mildew on walls and furniture. Condensation won't disappear on its own. There are times of year when it's more prevalent, but unless you fix the problem, the condensation will recur. One interesting fact is that the bright sunlight the next day can work to evaporate the moisture, but the reality is the evaporated moisture stays in the house, thus causing the house to stay too moist. The primary cause of condensation is a house with too much humidity in it. A quality dehumidifier, along with proper bathroom and even kitchen exhaust fans, (and ventilating the home if possible) can help to reduce the household humidity levels. Left untreated, mold and mildew can prove to be a health hazard for the residents. Plus, the costs of repair from damaged windows and walls can certainly eat away at your profits. If you test the home with a hygrometer and the relative humidity level is sitting above 60 percent, you certainly have a problem that needs to be dealt with.

I realize that none of these repairs and prevention devices will do much to add to your property value. Resale value won't go up because you have insulated your attic hatch or added a sensor to your bathroom exhaust fan. An appraiser simply doesn't care that you actively lower the humidity levels in your home and you regularly clean out your eavestroughs and gutters. He likely doesn't have a column to add value for your creation of a French drain diverting water away from the foundation. However, I can assure you that when the inevitable damages arise from NOT taking some of these steps, your resale or appraisal value will fall.

As a buy and hold investor, I really don't care too much about the resale values. Plus, I don't often re-appraise my properties anymore. However, I am still and always will be cautious about water or moisture entering into my units, as those problems can and will cost me time and money.

> *"True prevention is not waiting for bad things to happen,*
> *it's preventing them from happening in the first place."*
> *—Don McPherson*

SUCCESS STORY
Paul and Marlene Liberatore

Paul first decided the time was right to consider real estate investing around 2012. Unlike most new investors, Paul was then 64. He had spent a career as a premium contractor and saw so many investors and homeowners profit from his work, he decided that this was his time to build his own wealth.

Paul and Marlene have two adult sons who joined their dad in the family business and were also skilled contractors, however, they really hadn't built any significant wealth.

Paul made the decision to learn more about real estate investing and along with his oldest son, Alan, began attending a local investment club meeting. They had the skills to complete any job, but they didn't know what to buy. It was at one of those meetings they met me and also began learning from the Doors to Wealth team. Marlene explained that they were looking for someone who had already had some success in real estate investing. They weren't just looking for a Realtor to show them some properties, but someone who could help them along the entire process.

Before too long, they chose a bungalow with the option to convert it into a two-unit dwelling, but it would need extensive work to complete. The whole family still worked full time for other customers, so this project would take far longer than most typically take. However, they knew if they worked evenings and weekends, they could complete the project in a reasonable time.

Paul had had some success as a contractor and he and Marlene had some investments including owning two condos "free and clear," meaning there was no mortgage debt on them. However, Paul's motivation was not really to build more wealth for him and his wife, but to have something to leave for their sons and grandkids.

The amount of renovation work needed in the bungalow presented a significant roadblock, and because they were taking the building right back to the studs, it was not just one renovation, but essentially two. Despite the challenges, however, they never seriously considered selling the property and Paul kept driving the project, knowing that if they could build a quality, well-designed couple of units, they would have an asset for years to come.

None of Paul's friends, family, or colleagues had ever invested in real estate, so although they had done so many renovations for their clients, and they had the two condo units, owning multi unit investment real estate was new to them. But Paul knew that this could be a lasting legacy for his family.

Eventually, the project was complete and they got in two outstanding tenants. They were so pleased with the results that they wanted to do it again. It was then that they came across a unique four-unit building that needed significant work in every unit. This wasn't a traditional four-unit building; it was more like four separate townhomes under one roof. Two of them were three-bedroom and two were two-bedroom units. Marlene pointed out that as much work as the first one had been, this one would be at least twice that amount. But Paul was determined to go ahead.

The quality of work was at designer levels, but again they were determined to "do it right" to attract the best quality tenants and have less repair work afterwards. It was a slow process, but one by one they were able to move the exiting tenants out and complete an extensive renovation.

Unfortunately, Paul was diagnosed with cancer when he was 69. Despite his illness, he continued to move forward and quarterbacked the renovations, knowing the importance of completing these jobs. He oversaw all the work himself and even as he grew weaker you knew that you could always pop into the fourplex and see Paul puttering away on some project. Paul bravely fought the cancer for nearly two years, but at 71, in the summer of 2018, it became apparent that he was not going to beat the terrible disease.

Lisa and I had the chance to visit Paul a couple of weeks before he passed away. Although he was weaker, he still had spirit and determination. We chatted that day for about an hour, and it remains a conversation that I will never forget. Paul expressed his gratitude that we were able to help him and his family buy the two properties. He was proud of the fact that the properties had appreciated in value and he was able to leave a true legacy behind for his children. But I think it was Lisa and I that most benefited from that afternoon's conversation. Paul shared so many stories and reminders of what is truly important in life. It puts things in perspective; you don't need to spend every waking hour building and working. While it's important to build enough wealth for your future and have something to leave behind for your loved ones, at the end of the day, it is life's experiences that you remember most.

Today, Paul and Marlene's two sons, Alan and Ryan, manage the properties. They continue to work as full-time contractors. In fact, they have even hired a property manager to help find tenants and manage the day-to-day operations of the units. As such, other than an hour or two of paperwork a month, the properties now basically run themselves. In fact, they generate enough revenue to cover all their expenses including the property management fees. Any extra revenue to date has either gone back into renovating the property or paying down the mortgage. They wouldn't think about ever selling the units. Although they don't keep any of the cash flow from the buildings, they know they are accumulating significant wealth for themselves and their kids.

Alan and Ryan have done an excellent job in carrying the torch. In fact, they are now spending time teaching their teenage kids the importance of owning real estate. Marlene points out that it's getting tougher and tougher for kids these days to be able to afford real estate. The kids joke that the four of them can one day move into each unit in the fourplex and share the cooking and yard maintenance.

The grandkids are starting to get it. It's gratifying to see that the efforts of Paul attending the local real estate meetings, taking action, and buying properties is providing a lasting legacy for his family.

ARMCHAIR MINDSET PLAYBOOK

☂   Review and research flood plain maps and flooding history of the area that you are considering as a location you want to invest in. Don't assume that it will be disclosed at the time of purchase. Do your own due diligence.

☂   When "shopping" for insurance, consider evaluating the strength of the insurance company and their ability to withstand a catastrophic event. It is not always just about which rate is lowest.

☂   Eavestroughs, gutters and downspouts are often overlooked, but are vitally important in water prevention. Cracks, damage and blockages to them can lead to significant water damage inside your building.

CHAPTER 8

KEEP YOUR SANITY...PICK THE RIGHT TENANTS

"A wealthy person is simply someone who has learned to make money when they're not working."
—*Robert Kiyosaki*

I've said this before, and I will likely say it again throughout the book …before you buy, decide what type of tenant you want to have and find a property that will attract them.

I know I sound like a broken record (note to millennials…there once was a circular object known as a "record" that when placed on a "record player" would play music. Occasionally, the record had a scratch on it, and the same notes would repeat over and over), but I will say it again:

Buy a QUALITY PROPERTY.

In a QUALITY NEIGHBORHOOD.

That attracts QUALITY TENANTS.

And makes you QUALITY PROFITS.

MORE THAN CASH FLOW

Projected cash flow is an important measuring stick when determining the next property to buy. But it is not the only factor. Once upon a time, a sales representative in a city with dropping property values approached me about referring my clients to him as he could get them way better cash flow than they were currently receiving. I looked at his projections and saw that he was correct. However, he missed a few very key points that made me decide to stay away from that investment strategy.

#1. The 100-year-old properties were valued low. In some cases, under $100,000. Without having seen the units I was certain that the previous property owners had not been maintaining them to my standards and I would be faced with an expensive repair bill.

#2. The tenant profile he was pitching at was not the tenant profile I wanted. I am often amused how a Realtor can put together a projected set of numbers that bear no resemblance to reality. They will use top-line rental numbers assuming every unit is rented AND paying rent. They will show repairs, maintenance, and garbage removal as next to nothing.

#3. This property, after 100 years, is now worth $100,000. Even if the cash-flow projections are accurate and the repairs are minimal, this place hasn't really appreciated in value in a century. What makes me think that it will increase when I buy it? The big prize in the buy and hold game is appreciation, but if that is not there, the numbers, regardless of the cash flow just aren't as good.

I thanked the sales rep for reaching out but told him that the properties did not meet my property profile. I felt that the tenants they would attract wouldn't meet the level I was looking for—possibly they wouldn't even have jobs. The sales rep argued that focusing on tenants who were on social assistance was great because they "had to live somewhere" and the money was sent directly from the government to the landlord. But I was not swayed.

Insider Tip: In some provinces and states the tenant has control over whether the rental money is sent directly from the government institution to the landlord when on social assistance. Some "professional tenants" say they will have the money sent directly to the property owner, but once they move in, change it back to it being paid directly to the tenant. Then they don't pay the rent. Depending on your state or province, and also depending on your own diligence, it may take three to six months to evict that tenant, and the property owner will have no rental income during that time.

I love cash flow. I want my properties to pay ME dividends every month for the rest of my life. But buying a property in markets without the right fundamentals, especially ones with tremendous flaws, may cause you more effort than you want to take on. If you buy quality two-unit properties, with solid rental income and a great tenant profile, the cash flow will follow.

CASE STUDY
HORROR STORY: WHERE IS THAT SMELL COMING FROM?

I inherited a tenant from a property I acquired who was a hoarder and a slob. She had three kids and countless pets. I should have known to walk away when I was doing a walk-through of the unit and one of the cats attacked me. The cat literally clawed onto the back of my calf and bit into me. By the time the cat was ripped from my leg, I had small puncture wounds in my leg where the claws and teeth had punctured the skin.

Anyway, months later the rent payments stopped. I went to visit the property and was practically knocked over by the odor. To get rid of the tenant, I forgave past overdue rent and gave her a few dollars for moving costs. I just knew that every day she was in the property she was doing more damage to the place.

Once the family left, the major clean up began. We removed all the junk left behind, threw out carpets, and cleaned thoroughly. But we couldn't get rid of the smell. It was horrible. It was beyond horrible. We were down to the floorboards in some rooms and were even considering removing them too.

Meanwhile, in the same reno, I decided to change the furnace. A couple of the ducts needed to be moved slightly to accommodate the new furnace. It was during this work that the contractor I had working on the project felt liquid fall on his shoulder. Upon looking inside the duct, he found piles of dog and cat feces, along with urine stains. We later learned that the kids were assigned the task of cleaning up the pet mess and instead of picking it up and throwing it away, they would sweep it into the ductwork! This meant that I needed to tear out the entire ceiling of the lower unit to remove and replace all the ducts. After that, surprisingly, the smell went away.

There is a temptation to really want to make a difference in a community. If you fix up one property, it might create a chain reaction and then you're really on the ground floor of a true transformation. There are certainly examples of this happening. But in the investing world there is a saying:

PIONEERS GET SLAUGHTERED. SETTLERS PROSPER.

As tempting as it is to be the pioneer or innovator and see your vision realised in the community, the real winners in this game keep their investment strategy simple, predictable, and repeatable.

In real estate, we like to say that the three most important things to consider when buying a home are location, location, and location. When it comes to a quality investment property, this might not be a home or area where you would want to live and raise your family, but it might make for a wonderful investment property. Ensure that the real estate fundamentals work for this location. The ideal rental location may not be in the most expensive neighborhood or best school district but close to transit, shopping, and the tenant's employment. If you can own a property where the future tenant wants to live, it goes a long way to ensuring continual rent.

> *Insider Tip: There are many factors to consider when buying a property, but one way to assure that you will have regular rental demand is to buy a property that is close to everything. Check out the website www. walkscore.com and type in the address of the property you are looking at. This site looks at transit and offers a bike score and a walk score. It looks at the shops, restaurants, and attractions in the area and scores accordingly. There are occasional things it doesn't pick up, but it gives a good general assessment of the "walkability" of the location. The more central your property, the wider the net you can cast when seeking out the ideal tenant.*

TYPE AND AGE OF PROPERTY

In many towns and cities across North America, there are many downtown area properties originally built between 1910 and 1930. These properties can appear to be wonderful opportunities to get into real estate investing affordably as the purchase price on them can sometimes be 20 to 40 percent lower than the average home price in the city. However, remember that you are a savvy real estate investor and you realize that the property is dated, and may not have had extensive renovations done to it in over 50 years. It may have outdated electrical, plumbing, and windows, not to mention a kitchen and bathroom that haven't been touched in 50 to 100 years. This "cheaper" property could wind up costing you way more in the long run as the renovation costs wear away at your budget.

Of course, you can argue that the property has existed in this state for many years, why fix it now? A poorly renovated unit in a dilapidated building will never attract a premium or even a mid-range tenant. You will only attract a tenant who can't find anywhere else to live. Don't bother doing a credit or employment check as they likely won't have a job and their credit rating will suck. They probably need a place because their current landlord "is a jerk," and is kicking them out for lack of rent payments (the nerve of him). You can expect your property to take further abuse as they won't respect it.

Yes, I am stereotyping, but an afternoon or two of visiting the downtown core tenants will likely sour you from ever wanting to invest in those properties. You will have no problem chatting with these tenants in your afternoon visits as most aren't working. I like to bring newer investors that come with their children to these properties. The combined aroma of pet urine and body odor along with a marijuana fragrance scares them off in a hurry. The kids' reactions are especially priceless.

But let's say you have a strong appetite for a challenge. You want to take on the project as the price of the property is just too good to pass up. You effectively dispose of the problem tenants and set forth restoring the property. When completed, is this a place that your target renters are going to want to live? If all the homes surrounding it are also dilapidated, you are not likely going to be able to attract and retain quality tenants. Even if you can convince them to move in, once they see their neighbors and their kids interact with the street influences, there is an excellent chance that they will start seeking out another place to live.

SETTING THE RIGHT PRICE FOR MONTHLY RENT

I often hear stories of landlords who intentionally undercharge the rent (below market value). The reasons are varied, but the most common reason is that the landlord wants to have his choice of tenant, and feels that by lowering the asking price, he can pick and choose the tenant he wants. He will also choose to not raise the rent after the first year is completed, thus putting his rental even further behind.

> *Insider Tip: I ask property owners if they prefer their tenants over members of their own family. When they say, of course not, I then ask if they give their children $3,000-$5,000 a year as a gift. Most often, the answer is no. Then I explain that by intentionally undercharging the rent to the tenant, they have made a conscious decision to give them a $3,000-$5,000 gift ANNUALLY. Of course, the tenants may be nice enough people, but do they really appreciate the annual gift you are giving them? Typically, that answer is hell no.*

Property owners often think they can push out the raising of rents to another time. Another side effect of COVID is that some provincial and state governments are limiting the amount of rent that a rental housing provider can increase the rent for the upcoming year. Never miss an opportunity to raise your rent, as it might not be available at another time. Also, don't be afraid to charge market rents to your tenants. As long as you have a safe, legal, well-maintained dwelling unit, the tenants will want to stay.

WHEN THE AD IS LIVE...BE READY TO ACT

Don't post the ad, receive the leads, then get back to potential tenants on the weekend when it's convenient to you. Too many landlords and even property management companies contact their applicants once a day or LESS. Regardless of the quality of your unit, and the quantity of other rentals out there in your market, if you don't get back to your inquiring applicants, they WILL look elsewhere. We live in a "right now" world. After location and price, I can't think of anything as important as getting back to a potential applicant.

Remember, finding a quality tenant takes time. Don't fret over one more month of lost rent—wait for the tenant that meets your desired profile. If you followed through and bought the QUALITY PROPERTY in the QUALITY NEIGHBORHOOD, as tempting as it is, don't just take the first person who shows any interest and fills out the application.

Consider setting up a pre-screening questionnaire for every interested party. Sometimes applicants simply aren't a good fit for a particular unit. For example, if they say they're moving to the area for work but it turns out that's a good two to three hours away from your unit, then they're better off looking for a property in a town closer to their job. A few pre-screening questions can save you and the applicant a lot of time. You can even embed questions in the ad and then reach out only to the applicants who seem like they could be a decent fit, based on their responses.

Expect many people who contact you, fill out the pre-screening questions, and provide you with their complete set of information to NEVER answer the phone or call you back when you reach out to them. Potential tenants apply to many ads at the same time. Only the good, reliable ones, specifically the ones that you might really want to rent to, will call you back. Also, don't be surprised when you set up a series of appointments and the majority of them don't even show up. Try not to take it personally. Ask them how they would prefer to communicate with you—phone, text, email? What's the best time of day to communicate with them? Knowing all of this up front will save you time later on.

COUCH SURFING APPLICANTS

Applicants find their next rental by surfing the web, looking through available listings. This is not an age thing. With very few exceptions, everyone does it. Whether it be online dating, getting a new outfit, choosing what movie to watch, buying a house, or finding a rental to live in, most people today first see it online, and based on that, decide if they want to move forward or not. This is the new reality.

To attract the best candidates for your rental property, it is best to "dress up" your listing/advertisement with all of its best features, local landmarks, and make the effort to position your property as the ideal place for the applicant to next choose to live.

Post the maximum number of pictures allowed on the posting site. If the site allows you 10 photos, then USE 10 photos. If you can use video, do it. You don't need to have a professional videographer doing your photo shoot. In the past, we've done a walking tour of a unit, with the camera going and us talking about the features. Yeah, the first couple of times you do it, you're going to think it came out stupid. You may hate the sound of your voice on video but get over it. Adding video almost always increases the number of people wanting to see the unit. Plus, the applicant often makes comments about the unit once inside, as if they have been there before. The video acts almost like their first walkthrough.

Remember, if your ad only attracts a small number of rental candidates, the chances of you attracting a suitable tenant is reduced. By making the listing as good as possible, you are casting that wider net, and having more people look at your rental property. Just like any other commodity, the more demand you can create the more picky you can be on the supply end. A good advertisement can lead to a shorter search period, better applicants and even higher rents received.

> *Insider Tip: Spending a little time and money to best present your unit for photos and video will allow you to market your unit efficiently again and again. Once the current tenant moves out, you can use the photos you had done originally and immediately post the ad.*

WHERE TO ADVERTISE

Gone are the days when property owners spent hundreds of dollars advertising in the local paper. Every day the owner had to spend more as the paper was thrown out daily. Today, we use sites like Facebook Marketplace, Facebook groups specializing in local rental units, Kijiji, Zumper, and local newspaper online classifieds, amongst others. If you are using a property manager, ask them where they post. I'm certain that over the next decade, a number of new advertising platforms will become available. You can even pay to boost your ad. Spending $10-$20 will tremendously enhance the chances of reaching more people and finding your targeted tenant. However, nothing you can read here, or in other books on this subject can match interacting with other savvy investors in the market you are looking to invest in and asking what they have found successful.

> *Insider Tip: Pretend that you are a new resident to your market and are looking for a place to rent. Go online and look for the best group of properties that might meet the tenant profile you are trying to replicate. There is nothing wrong with calling one or two of the ads and introducing yourself as an investor in that market and letting them know how much you admire their listing and their property. Ask the property owner, whose ad and property you respect, some questions. If they are willing to engage with you, perhaps their insight will be most helpful.*

PROPERTY MANAGERS

A good property manager (PM) earns their salary by maximizing rents and minimizing vacancies and lost rent. If you are the hands-on type of person and want to be involved in the day-to-day operations of your real estate business then you may not require a property manager. However, if you loathe the idea of battling with tenants and that fear has been the main reason why you're holding back from purchasing potential cash-flow generating, wealth-building real estate, then a property manager is likely a smart call.

Most of us are somewhere in between.

In our case, we have no problem dealing with tenant issues or finding the right tenant for a property. However, because of distance and our own schedules, having a PM makes a lot of sense for us for some of our portfolio.

Yes, the PM might lower my cash flow, however, I am more confident that the place isn't falling apart and I can spend my available time on more revenue production or in more relaxing ways. Either way, I can focus on what I want to do rather than what I have to do.

I am often asked, what should I look for in a property manager? To me the perfect PM has the following attributes.

1. They own some cash flow-generating properties themselves;

2. They understand your tenant profile and strive to meet those requirements;

3. They have systems in place to monitor the property on a semi-regular basis; and

4. They have a team of contractors and handymen on call when needed.

Some PMs offer a "menu" of services. Perhaps you want to do the repairs and renos yourself but need help finding the right tenant. Perhaps you want to work with the tenants on an ongoing basis, but need assistance collecting rent and paying bills.

One of my mentors often asks a crowded room to raise their hands if they do their own property management. Half the room raises their hands. Then he says to keep them raised until it really starts to hurt. That's how it feels to manage your own properties, he says.

Sorry, I'm too busy to move forward in that project, I have to go mow my tenant's lawn!

If you have just one or two properties, time to deal with minor issues, and don't mind the "stress" of dealing with a problem tenant situation, then hiring a PM might not be necessary. However, if you have any intention of growing your portfolio, you will eventually have to give up property management from your own day-to-day activities.

Think about it this way. In real estate investing there are jobs worth $10-$25 an hour, there are jobs worth $100 an hour, and there are jobs worth $1,000 an hour or more. Working with your Realtor and looking at opportunities could allow you to find a deal worth thousands of dollars. But if you need to cancel that appointment because you need to show one of your vacant units to a potential tenant, clean an apartment, or do some minor repair work, you are choosing to save tens of dollars while losing out on the opportunity to make thousands of dollars.

> **Insider Tip:** *Make a list of the things you do on an ongoing basis for your real estate portfolio. Put it in a column format. Next to it, write*

> *down the level of time you have spent on this task over the past few months.*
>
> *Score it a 1 if it hasn't taken up much time, a 2 if it took a bit of time, and a 3 if it took a large percentage of your time. Next to that, write down the level of importance this task takes in the building of your real estate portfolio and its profitability. (Again, score it a 1, 2, or 3).*
>
> *Finally, write down a 10 if someone else did this job for you if that worker charged you $10-$50 an hour. Write down 100 if the task was worth $100 an hour or more. Finally, write down 1,000 if the task was worth $1,000 an hour or more.*
>
> *Then begin the process of divesting yourself from the "10" jobs, especially if they are low in importance and higher in time spent. Many feel that property management falls into this category.*

DON'T BE A PLUSH TOY

Compassion, understanding, and "having a heart" are all good character traits to have in life, but sometimes it doesn't serve you well in this industry. Sometimes, you just can't be too soft and squishy. Either during the tenant selection, or after the tenant moves in, it's good to be fair and honest, but there are times to remember that you're still running a business. It's OK to feel bad for a tenant who lost their job, hurt their back, or has a mother who is very sick. We should absolutely have empathy for their plight. But you simply can't agree to delay or lower their rent, as you too have bills to pay. If you feel unable or unwilling to provide a delinquency of rent notification, days after their beloved dog just died, then perhaps you should consider hiring a property manager.

TENANT SELECTION...TELL ME WHAT YOU WANT, WANT YOU REALLY, REALLY WANT.

With apologies to the Spice Girls, let's look deeper into the tenant-seeking process and try to find the formula for finding the best tenants. Although I don't discount the "I have a good feeling about this applicant" vibe or the "My Spidey-senses are telling me to stay away from this one" instincts, it likely makes far more sense to base your decision-making on facts. Consider the following in your decision:

1. **Credit score**

   Unless you have been living under a rock or isolated from the rest of society, you will already know what a credit score is. We often look beyond just the actual score number. Because many of your tenant applicants have very few "hits" against the credit, one late payment or "mistake" can throw them into a terrible score. The most common indiscretion is forgetting to pay out a cell phone bill. Often the person resents the extra charges to close out a phone or service and chooses not to pay or moves and kind of avoids the payment. Often they owe less than $200. The company, after not getting their money, just throws it over to collections and royally screws the person's credit score. Even after repayment is made, that one bad debt could take years to bounce back from. But one bad Fido bill three years ago doesn't, in itself, make the tenant a bad risk. As a property owner, you would obviously dive deeper. Of course, if the applicant is behind on multiple credit cards and is nearly maxed out, that is a bad sign.

   I have often been asked if it is really necessary to incur the expense of doing a credit check. To make it simpler for those of you who like visual explanations, I put the answer into a circle graph.

IS CHECKING THE TENANT'S CREDIT SCORE A GOOD IDEA?

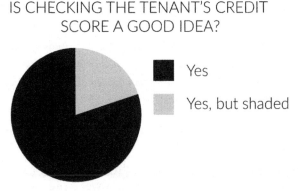

Table 3 : Is it good to check your tenant's credit score?

To be clear, in the graph, the answer was YES. I just broke it down into two sections for humor's sake. I don't care if it's your high school buddy, some couple with a solid six-figure income, or Grandma Rose (OK maybe Grandma MIGHT get a pass).

If you have not checked your own credit score for more than a year, it might be a good time to do it. As you look to build your portfolio, maintaining a strong credit score is essential in allowing you to obtain the financing you desire.

Lenders check your credit score to determine your credit worthiness. The main credit sites are Equifax and TransUnion, but there are also third-party sites out there. It's important to pay for the full credit report, and not just the number, to verify if some of the information is not accurate. You take a physical once a year or so to verify your health, you go to the dentist often enough to verify your dental health. Consider checking your credit score once in a while to verify your credit health.

CASE STUDY
WHAT IS IN YOUR CREDIT REPORT?

I just took my own advice and did a credit check. It cost me about $20. Although my credit score ranked as "Excellent" there were some pretty glaring errors. First, my home address was wrong. It listed one of my investment properties as my residence. This likely happened when I was getting a mortgage, and the lender made an error (damn you, Bank of Montreal). Second, my employer was wrong. It switched details of my current employer and former employers. Thankfully, there were no obvious mistakes in my actual credit history, however, it was possible that because of the number of mortgages I have, and the size of my line of credit, my overall credit score may have been affected.

It's important to really understand how credit scores are created. There is no magic formula. When a credit score is sub-optimal, knowing how a credit score is created might give you a better handle on why it is lower. Then you can decide if the lower score is one that is acceptable to you, or one that should make you walk away.

HOW CREDIT SCORES ARE CALCULATED

This information is directly from Equifax.ca, which offers some excellent general information.

There are many different scoring models. Here is a general breakdown of the factors the models consider:

PAYMENT HISTORY: 35 PERCENT

Your credit history includes information about how you have repaid the credit you have already been extended on credit accounts such as credit cards, lines of credit, retail department store accounts, installment loans, auto loans, student loans, finance company accounts, home equity loans, and mortgage loans for primary, secondary, vacation, and investment properties.

In addition to reporting the number and type of credit accounts that you've paid on time, this category also includes details on late or missed payments, public record items, and collection information. Credit scoring models look at how late your payments were, how much was owed, and how recently and how often you missed a payment. Your credit history will also detail how many of your credit accounts are delinquent in relation to all your accounts on file. For example, if you have 10 credit accounts (known as "tradelines" in the credit industry) and you've had a late payment in five of those accounts, that ratio may impact your credit score.

USED CREDIT VERSUS AVAILABLE CREDIT: 30 PERCENT

A key part of your credit score analyzes how much of your total available credit is being used on your credit cards, as well as any other revolving lines of credit. A revolving line of credit is a type of loan that allows you to borrow, repay, and then reuse the credit line up to its available limit.

Also included in this factor is the total line of credit or credit limit.

This is the maximum amount you could charge against a particular credit account, say $2,500 on a credit card.

CREDIT HISTORY: 15 PERCENT

This section of your credit file details how long your credit accounts have existed. The credit score calculation typically includes both how long your oldest and most recent accounts have been open. In general, creditors like to see that you've been able to properly handle credit accounts over a period of time.

PUBLIC RECORDS: 10 PERCENT

Those who have a prior history of bankruptcy or have had collection issues or other derogatory public records may be considered risky. The presence of these events may have a significant negative impact on a credit score.

INQUIRIES: 10 PERCENT

Whenever an individual's credit file is accessed for any reason, the request for information is logged on the file as an inquiry. Inquiries require the consent of the individual and some may affect the individual's credit score calculation although this only applies to those related to active credit seeking (such as applying for a new loan or credit card). These inquiries are known in industry jargon as "hard pulls" or "hard hits" on your credit file. The inquiry may be the leading indicator, the first sign of financial distress that appears on the credit file. Of course, not every inquiry is a sign of financial difficulty, and only a number of recent inquiries, in combination with other warning signals on the credit file should lead to a significant decline in a credit score.

Let me dispel some myths often associated with credit scores:

- Checking your score personally will NOT rank as a hit on your credit score and will NOT affect your score in any way.

- When lenders or landlords do a check on your credit worthiness, it does NOT in itself "kill your credit score," as inquiries only represent 10 percent of your entire score.

- If your score is poor, it is not because you just added a credit card and it required a credit check.

- Choosing to tear up and cancel all your credit cards may not help your credit worthiness. No credit is actually more worrisome to a lender than mediocre credit.

Insider Tip: *Improve Your credit score*

- *If you are creating a credit history or are looking to improve your credit score, consider adding a credit card where you have to provide the lender with a deposit equal to your credit limit. Make sure that you make each payment. Two different credit cards like that with six to 12 months of payment history will turn your credit score around in a hurry.*

- *Lowering your credit limit can HURT your credit score. In fact, if you have a balance on a credit card or home equity line of credit, inquire to see if they will raise the limit. If the credit card has a $10,000 limit and a balance of $8,000, this will work against your credit score. If the lender is willing to increase your limit to $20,000, the $8,000 balance is now well under 50 percent of the balance and as long as you are making your payments, it is a good thing. The used credit versus available credit category represents 30 percent of the entire credit score, so it's a big deal.*

- *Thoroughly look through your credit report for old credit cards that are still active. A $100 balance on your Home Depot card from 2015, now in collections, can greatly affect your score. If there are credit cards out there that are still active that you completely forgot about, consider getting rid of them. Although unlikely, if your identity is ever compromised, you might never know about that Brick, Target, or Costco credit card from years ago.*

In order to complete a credit check on tenant applicants you will need to register for this service. You simply can't run a credit check without getting an application back from the tenant and their signed authorization allowing you to do that check. In Canada, it's important to note that if you do a credit check, you must keep it on file for the next seven years.

2. **Income Source and Other Monthly Debts and Expenses**

A good tenant applicant must not just have the money for the first and last months rent, and any other deposits if possible, but must have the wherewithal to pay you every month going forward, as long as they live in your property. Seeing statements of employment (employment letters), pay stubs, bank account statements (seeing the money going in), or any other way to ensure that the tenant has a regular source of income is the first step.

But remember: NOT EVERYONE TELLS THE TRUTH. If I want to be a bad guy and steal from you, I'm not going to tell you I'll be robbing you over the next few months. If I intend to get into your property and not pay you the expected rent, I may not tell you the truth about my income. Verify, verify, verify. Calling the "contact" the applicant provides you may be acceptable but consider diving deeper. Consider calling their place of employment and asking for the person. If they say, "Who? No one by that name works here," you may have a problem. Look up the phone number of the company online and call that number versus any number given on an application to ensure you are not getting 'a friend's cell number' versus the real company.

It's also a good idea to determine if the applicant has full-time employment, is permanent part-time, or is on a contract. I'm not saying you should exclude someone who is on a contract, but you should ask them how likely their contract is to continue, and if it ends, what alternatives they have for future employment and income.

I don't completely exclude applicants who are on social programs for their sole income, however, it is absolutely worth noting that tenants who work outside of the home are in your property primarily in the evenings and weekends only. Tenants who do not work, or who work from home, are ALWAYS in the property and the unit will typically have more wear and tear in it over time. Two final comments. (1) The vast majority of tenants we have selected over the years have had full time employment. (2) The vast majority of tenant complications we have experienced over the years came from tenants who were not employed outside of the unit.

Lending institutions have a measure of whether they expect the tenant to be able to pay them back with a mortgage or loan. This is called a **Total Debt Service Ratio** (TDS). It's a way for financial lenders to determine the proportion of gross income that a borrower has historically spent on housing-related and other similar payments.

Lenders consider each potential borrower's property taxes, credit card balances, and other monthly debt obligations to calculate the ratio of income to debt, and then compare that number to the lender's benchmark for deciding whether or not to extend credit.

The formula for calculating TDS is:

(Housing Costs + Other Debt Payments)/Gross Family Income

> *"A TDS ratio helps lenders determine whether a borrower can manage monthly payments and repay borrowed money. When applying for a mortgage, lenders look at what percentage of a borrower's income would be spent on the mortgage payment, real estate taxes, homeowner's insurance, association dues, and other obligations. Lenders also figure in what portion of income is already used for paying credit card balances, student loans, child support, auto loans, and other debts showing up on a borrower's credit report. A stable income, timely bill payment, and a strong credit score are not the only factors considered in being extended a mortgage. Borrowers with higher TDS ratios are more likely to struggle to meet their debt obligations than borrowers with lower ratios." (Source: Investopedia.com)*

We choose to also follow this method when selecting a tenant. If the rent we want to charge represents more than 33 percent of their total gross income for the family, we start to get nervous about their ability to pay us each month. If we combine this figure with large balances on their credit cards and one or two car loans, we begin to think this might just be a disaster ready to happen. With the bills piling up, and the credit card companies calling non-stop, the applicant may just choose to not make a rent payment or two.

Insider Tip: As mentioned, lenders use TDS all the time. When calculating a borrower's other debt payments, they look to the minimum monthly payments as fixed expenses. Lowering your minimum or consolidating to one larger balance with a lower combined minimum will improve your TDS.

As for mortgage payments, paying down the mortgage with accelerated payments actually HURTS your TDS. The calculation is based on what you pay each month, so by paying the balance off faster than you need to, the amount is scored against your TDS ratio (it raises your minimum monthly payment). Ensure that you are not making biweekly payments, but monthly; biweekly payments will mean 26 payments, or the equivalent of 13 months in one year (i.e., an accelerated payment).

If you have had a mortgage for a number of years, you can ask your lender to extend the amortization to the maximum allowed. Let me explain. A mortgage that was originally for 25 years on a property you have owned for seven years now has an amortization of 18 years left before the balance is paid off. By extending the amortization, in this example back to 25 years, it will effectively lower the monthly payments and IMPROVE your TDS.

With the low interest rates found today, this is "cheap money" and there is less of a need to pay it back quickly. This strategy, when used on your investment properties will effectively increase your monthly cash flow as the mortgage payment expense will be reduced. If you still want to pay down the mortgage with the extra funds, most lenders allow one-time payments of 5–10 percent of the balance of the mortgage. This one-time payment will not affect the TDS negatively.

3. Tenant History

This check may very well be the most important, yet it's often the most difficult to verify. The applicant will provide you with details of their current residence and hopefully previous accommodations. It's imperative that you contact the property owners or the property management company to get a verification of the occupancy and an opinion of how they were as tenants.

Word of warning Part One. If the tenant is an "asshole" and the current landlord dreams about the day they leave, it is not in their best interest to tell the complete and absolute truth about this lovely human being.

In the case of my "feces in the ductwork" tenant, I was called by a future potential landlord and asked for my opinion of her. I simply stated that I was doing a major renovation on the property, and the house had to be vacated while the reno was going on. I failed to mention that the reno was made necessary because of their actions and that they owed me thousands in rent that I will never get back. It must have slipped my mind.

If possible, contact the landlord two or more accommodations ago. They have no vested interest in lying to you. If someone called about this tenant today, I would have a nice little story to tell them.

Some of my colleagues even pop by the property to meet the tenant in their current home, to "get some paperwork signed," such as approval to do a credit check or something. If the place is a disaster and you're afraid to step inside, no matter how good the TDS and credit score are, they're not renting to them.

Insider Tip: If they were a former homeowner, contact your Realtor friend (we all have one) and ask to see the listing of the house they sold. If the photos look good, that makes me happy. I have previously even called the listing agent of the house they sold. Most Realtors will share the state of the home and worthiness of the potential tenant.

If the reason why the tenant had to move was because the home was sold, again contact the Realtor and get the inside scoop on how the tenant behaved. If they were reasonable during this difficult time for them, then they are likely a good tenant. If they were aggressive, sabotaged the process, and left the place a mess, it would be really nice to know that.

Word of Warning Part Two. Just because they put a name down as their landlord, doesn't mean that this person is actually their landlord. If your "Spidey senses" detect potential foul play, call from a blocked number and try to catch the "landlord" in a lie. One of my colleagues who was uncertain of the landlord's identity called back the next day under a different name and number saying he was a real estate investor asking if the "landlord" was interested in selling his investment property. When the guy said he had no investment properties, my colleague knew that he had caught the lie.

4. **Social Media and Internet Verification**

This is more "hit and miss" but worth the effort. Is the applicant a convicted felon? Does the applicant post hate messages on their social media platforms or are they simply angry at everything? Did the tenant say they don't smoke, yet you search and find multiple photos of them smoking up a storm? Is their Facebook page full of tributes to the marijuana plant?

By typing in the applicant's name on Google, Facebook, and Instagram you can see if any "red flags" pop up. This is no time to be prudish; the applicant may not be worthy of dating your son or daughter, but they may make an excellent tenant.

Some landlords ask for their prospective tenants' social media profile pages during the application process. We have personally stopped doing this as sometimes "good tenants" were taken aback by this request as an invasion of their privacy. It's up to you, of course. Some property owners take the approach that if they don't want to fill out the entire application, they're likely trying to hide something. That may also be true.

5. **What's Their Story?**

We like to know why an applicant is planning on leaving their current place. By asking this question, we have had some very interesting answers. The more they talk, the more they usually reveal.

It's an old trick in interviews, but often effective. Don't interrupt the applicant when they're speaking, and in some cases don't say anything at all. The applicant will fill the silence with more information.

- "The house is completely filled with bed bugs." (That likely means they will be bringing the bugs with them.)

- "The landlord is a slumlord." Do you believe that? (There are often two sides to a story. If it's an adversarial situation, I start to get nervous.)

- "Is the place available this weekend? I need a place to live." (There better be a damn good reason why they need to move in a couple of days. Good tenants are rarely days away from being homeless.)

- "They wouldn't let me smoke my medical marijuana." (Yeah, me neither.)

- "My boyfriend and his two kids moved in, so there wasn't enough space in my one-bedroom apartment with my two kids as well." (Meanwhile we are renting a two-bedroom unit. Way too small for two adults and four kids.)

- "We couldn't afford the rent there." (Our place is $100 more expensive a month. How can they afford it?)

6. Household Pets

In some provinces and states, even if a tenant signs a document saying they don't have pets, and will never have pets in the unit, they are permitted to walk in their two dogs, three cats, snake, and hamster the day they are handed the key. Because of that, instead of fighting the pet onslaught, consider going about things differently.

With close to 15 years in the retail pet industry, and a lifelong pet owner and lover, we tell applicants right from the start in our advertisements that we are pet friendly and so are our rental units. We promote the vinyl click flooring, which is great for cleaning up liquids of all kinds. We highlight our enclosed back yard so the dog can run around without worry.

We tell people that we have a Jack Russell TERROR and that our little beast is a trouble-maker, etc. Then we ask them what pets they have (even before they disclose that they have pets). Because we promote the pet aspect, we attract the premier pet-owning tenant population. They don't want to lie on their application. We have got some really good people to rent our units this way.

However, if they talk about the pets they own and it's beyond our comfort zone (aggressive breed dogs, waaaay too many cats, a 60-gallon aquarium of fish, etc.), then we can weed out that applicant.

7. **When in Doubt, Ask for a Guarantor**

A newly married couple with some spotty credit in the past could be awesome tenants, but if you base the decision only on the credit score, you might miss out on some real opportunities. If you meet an applicant you have a good feeling about, you like their income source, and you think they will take care of your home but their credit score isn't great, ask them if they have someone who can act as guarantor, someone who's prepared to step up and cover any missing rental payments or damages in the event that they don't pay up.

That final guarantee can get a decent applicant over the line and allow them to be your next tenant.

Insider Tip: Never, ever tell the applicant too much detail of why you didn't select them. Human rights regulations are so stringent today that informing them why they weren't chosen could open you up to legal action. Obvious "no-no" reasons are things which are not relevant to the process such as religion, sex, race, or political or sexual orientation. But even making a comment that you thought they were too young, or they need to have a job, or a host of other reasons can get you into

> *trouble. It's always best to simply say that you've chosen to go in a different direction and thank them for their interest.*

If you are still reading this . . .

CONGRATULATIONS! I haven't scared you off yet. The good news is that if you have chosen your property wisely and done your due diligence during the tenant selection, the risk of a bad tenant is quite low.

Offer quality properties to good people who will take care of your place, pay you for the privilege of providing them with safe shelter, and actually pay down your mortgage.

If you have hung around other investors for more than a minute, you will likely hear "war stories" of the worst experiences they have had as a landlord. It's almost like a badge of honor to share your worst tales and gross out the other participants in the conversation. My "feces in the ductwork" story always makes me a contender for grossest tale. But when we put our Realtor hats back on, and ask the crowd, "Who wants to sell their properties as we're looking for a few listings?" the room goes suddenly quiet.

You will hear me say this in other parts of the book, but the real win in real estate is in the HOLD. Despite their protests, concerns, and complaints, investors of cash-flow-generating real estate understand that the longer they hold onto their properties, the more wealth they will amass. Attracting and retaining quality tenants is a fundamental part of that. I don't want to dismiss the challenges associated with being a property owner and residential housing provider, however, remembering the "why" of WHY you are doing this puts into perspective the purpose for embarking on this (sometimes) crazy adventure.

"Be excellent to each other and party on, dudes."
—*Bill & Ted's Excellent Adventures (Also known as the first Ted Talk)*

SUCCESS STORY
Winter Ng and Sophia Lee

Winter and Sophia were both born in Hong Kong. They grew up and were educated there. They made the decision to come to Canada for more opportunities and a better life. When they settled in 1992, they were primarily focused on starting up their careers in physiotherapy.

Their first real estate purchase, as with most of us, was a house for them both to live in. No one in either of their families had ever been a real estate investor, so they simply did not consider investing in a property outside of their residence.

In the early 2000s, they had an opportunity to invest in a preconstruction condo. Friends warned them about the perils of being a landlord, so they were afraid of holding on to the properties. When the units were finally ready, they quickly sold them and did make a little bit of money, as the market in Toronto was rising. However, they also realized that this type of investing was more speculative. Plus, over time the cost to manage the properties would be higher than the rental income they could generate from them, which they didn't want. Although they did make money on these transactions, they were still hesitant about being landlords.

Fast forward to 2011, nearly 20 years after moving to Canada, with a successful physiotherapy business, a primary residence that was nearly paid off, and some retirement investments in stocks and mutual funds, and Sophia felt the time was right to consider real estate investing again.

Sophia did her research. She read Rich Dad, Poor Dad by Robert Kiyosaki and Real Estate Investing in Canada by Don R. Campbell. She borrowed all the books from the library about real estate investing. She went to her local bookstore and purchased and read everything they had on the subject. It was in that research that she discovered the Real Estate Investment Network (REIN) and other networking meet-ups. The whole process of research took more than six months. When she was finally confident, she convinced Winter that investing in real estate was the "correct step" to take for their futures to build wealth.

By the end of 2011, they had made their first two-unit purchase, a legal turnkey property that they could rent out right away. But they didn't stop there. Over time, they began to focus on doing renovations on some of their units and went through the conversion process with the city inspectors. Over and over again they repeated the process using funds from their principal residence and from their retirement savings in other investments. By 2016, they were up to 16 two-unit properties.

Like all real estate investors, they had some bumps along the way. There were times when the legalization process posed some major challenges. Having as many properties as they have, it will come as no surprise that they have had some pretty serious tenant issues over the years. Recently, one tenant chose to turn their unit into a rooming house to hold illegal immigrants. Fortunately, because they have systems in place, they were able to evict the tenant and re-rent it.

They spend about 30 –40 hours a month on their portfolio, depending on if they have vacancies. They manage everything themselves and seldom have any serious problems. Winter and Sophia are meticulous in their organization. They have a daily maintenance schedule and visit their properties often. When they find something in need of repair, they just do it, or hire someone who can fix it. They certainly don't want the burden of any deferred maintenance issues. The rest of the time is spent on admin, banking, and bookkeeping.

Real estate investing has had an incredible impact on their family's net worth. With the cash flow, mortgage pay down, and appreciation over the years, many of their investments have more than tripled in the years since they bought them. This was especially important as just a few years after they started investing, federal programs changed, directly affecting their physiotherapy practice and essentially crushing much of their business. Had they not been already investing, one or both of them may have had to take a position at another practice, working for someone else. But the wealth and freedom that came from real estate investing allowed them to continue in their practice part time, with less need to depend on the income that came from their original primary income.

Millions of first-generation immigrants now living in North America see their early immigration experience as both an asset and hinderance. Other than a strong education, Winter and Sophia really didn't land in their adopted country with much. In their own words, they "started from scratch." They both had a work visa, a strong work ethic, and a desire to succeed in their new country. In Hong Kong, there was a culture of buying real estate and in fact, many of their family members and friends had bought property to live in.

In fact, both sets of parents followed them to North America, and Winter and Sophia accommodated them in their family home by utilizing their basement and dining room. Along with their two children, the three generations living under one roof may have been crowded at times, but in their culture "it's what you do."

When it came to real estate investing they came with no special skills, training, or wealth. The research Sophia did only got them so far. It was only after they attended seminars and meet-ups and networked with other like-minded investors and real estate professionals that they felt comfortable in moving forward.

Looking back, they are happy with everything they bought. In fact, they plan to hold on to these properties into their retirement years. They see their portfolio as a big part of their children's inheritance. Their biggest regret is simply not buying more when they had the opportunities. They feel they really missed out at times because they didn't want to spend that extra couple of thousand dollars on a property and they were never interested in joint venturing with other parties. With the declared income they had at that time, and a different set of mortgage rules, they certainly could have grown their portfolio even larger.

Today you can still find Winter and Sophia attending local meet-ups and learning and networking with other like-minded investors. They may not receive as many new nuggets of knowledge in these meetings as they did back when they started out, but they are always available to share their experiences with the next generation of investors.

 ARMCHAIR MINDSET PLAYBOOK

☂ Buy a QUALITY property, in a QUALITY neighborhood, that attracts QUALITY tenants, and makes you QUALITY profits.

☂ When advertising for a prospective tenant, when the ad is live, be ready to act. The best tenant applicants won't wait around for you to call them back no matter how nice your place is.

☂ Spending a little time and money to best present your unit for photos and video will allow you to market your unit effectively again and again.

☂ Understanding credit scores is not that complicated. Knowing how to quickly improve your score can go a long way to improving your chances to getting that premium rate mortgage.

☂ Total Debt Service Ratio (TDS) is an effective measurement to predict if the tenant will have the ability to pay their rent. If you are looking to borrow more funds, there are ways to manipulate your TDS to allow you to qualify for a new investment property.

☂ Asking for a guarantor for a younger tenant or one with a spotty credit history is an added protection to ensure that you will be compensated for any missed rent or damages to the unit.

CHAPTER 9

PREPARING THE RIGHT LEASE

*"Don't go into business with the sole objective of making a lot
of money. If you put service, quality, and customer
satisfaction first, the money will follow."*
—Paul Clitheroe

As I have said already, the main objective of this book is to convince you to take action. There is a vast number of real estate-related books that focus on "finding the deal" and seeking joint venture money partners, but what I really want to give you here are action points and steps you can take and subject matter you can focus on for tenancy leases that you can use right away.

But first the disclaimer: I am not a lawyer or a paralegal. I am not making any claim that any clause I suggest will hold up in a landlord/tenant board hearing. Being from Ontario, it's possible that a few of these categories simply won't apply in your market, so it is ALWAYS recommended that you get knowledgeable, local legal help when creating your leases and to understand the laws in your area. It surprises me how little attention real estate courses give to the discussion of a lease. This document sets the tone for the relationship with your future tenant. This person or people, if agreed upon, will likely give you TENS of thousands of dollars over the next few years. They will be occupying your most valuable asset and in return you will be providing them with safe shelter—one of the fundamental needs of all human beings. To just say, "Let's wing it," to this stranger seems odd to me. But one day's visit to a landlord/tenant board dispute hearing will show you that a remarkable number of landlord/tenant disputes arise simply due to there being no lease or an illegal lease.

What follows is a checklist of items and ideas that should be accounted for in your lease. However, please note that no matter how much you research and prepare, and no matter how many people you talk to who are active investors, there will ALWAYS be something that arises that isn't covered in the lease. It will never, ever be perfect. The key is to put together a quality lease and put it into use.

As US General George Patton once said, "A good plan violently executed now is better than a perfect plan executed next week." The key is to get that "good plan," and that simply doesn't mean to "wing it" and throw something together.

Some states and provinces have created standardized leases. I think that is a good thing. There needs to be a minimum standard in all leases, to protect both the tenant and the landlord. But, even in regions that demand the standardized lease, the ability exists to include an attachment or a schedule to the lease that includes other terms not currently found in that original lease.

Keep in mind, you can't negate any of the terms or rights found in the original lease with a clause in the attachment. Rather, attachments can be used to provide depth and clarity in the future landlord/tenant relationship.

Here are some highlights of situations you should consider when preparing your lease for future tenants to sign. The more protections you create and provisions you deal with, the less likely something will happen for which you don't have a pre-prepared solution in place.

- How is the tenant expected to pay you the rent each month? You may be restricted from demanding the payment in a certain method. However, you can insist that it is up to the tenant to provide payment on a particular day. You should not be travelling around the area trying to collect your rent. STOP THE MADNESS! Even if you have just one property, and one tenant, treat your business LIKE a business. Create a system of collecting the rent where it is the tenant's responsibility to pay you.

- What do you do if you get an NSF cheque? What is your time worth? Have a fee structure in place in the event that a tenant starts bouncing cheques.

- How will you handle subletting? Address it right in the lease. The subtenant must be approved by the property owner PRIOR to them taking over the lease and moving in.

- What is the tenant actually renting? Spell it out right in the lease. What space is just for them? What common space can they share? How many parking spots do they have? Do they have access to the garage, backyard, shed, or storage locker?

- Can they run a business in the unit? You may have restrictions in your residential insurance regarding the operation of a day care or hair salon. Spell out the restrictions in the lease.

- Who's actually living in your property? Get the name of every occupant, adult, child, and pet. By getting multiple adults to sign a lease, it helps ensure there will be additional parties to pursue if things go bad in the future. It is also necessary to know should there ever be a fire, you can tell the emergency services there are X occupants and X pets.

- How are the utility expenses being handled? This is a large, ongoing expense. Understanding this in the beginning is essential. We ALWAYS want our tenants paying the utilities. It is a variable expense that can really eat away at the profits and the cash flow.

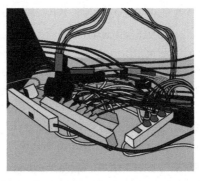

A quick visual inspection of your units can spot hazards before they become a bigger issue

- Do you want to have final say in what appliances can be used in your premises? Are you OK if the tenant brings in more appliances? How about a green house?

- Have you spelled out the landlord's and tenant's obligations for duty of care? A QUALITY tenant will expect that the property owner maintains the property in the event that something goes wrong. These are things that a diligent landlord is expected to do and it is appreciated by a potential tenant. Meanwhile, the tenant should be restricted from doing any significant alterations and renovations to the unit without permission from the landlord. Help set the tone that abuse of the property shall not be tolerated, but in turn, you will be there to maintain the building. There should also be clauses in place preventing cluttering of common areas or fire exits.

- Is there a provision allowing you access to the unit in the event of an emergency? A tenant should expect that their domain is their safe space and although you own the building, you may only enter the unit after providing proper notification. However, there are certain times when allowance must be made for the health and safety of the residents, and/or the preservation of the property is at risk. In those rare circumstances, the landlord should have the right to enter the building without proper notice provided. A QUALITY tenant will appreciate the attention to detail and concern in such a scenario.

- The laundry facilities are for the tenant's use only. You don't want it being used to clean the neighborhood's clothes or perhaps for commercial uses. State that right at the beginning.

- Have you spelled out what the tenant is expected to do with their garbage? Although it may seem obvious to most, we now always spell out when the garbage and recycling dates are for that property. We let it be known that the tenant is not permitted to store their garbage in sheds or garages, which may attract rodents and insects. Any debris in the yard must be removed by the tenant immediately.

- Is there any provision in place to deal with noise concerns?

In multiunit buildings, noise is often the most common complaint between tenants. Although occasional noise is not unusual, excessive noise and noise late in the evening is unacceptable. If the tenant has guests over, and the guest is the "guilty party" of the noise or disturbance, the tenant who invited the guest is ultimately responsible.

- Did you spell out that the tenant can't change the lock without permission? We want to have a copy of every lock to every one of our buildings. There are times when locks do need to be changed, so let us, as the landlord pay for and replace that lock. QUALITY tenants don't change the locks on a whim.

- Did you restrict non-vehicles from occupying the parking spaces provided? Yes, the parking spaces have been assigned to the tenant. However, that doesn't mean the occupant can use that space to store a boat, RV, dumpster, trash, or anything else. Limiting the use of the parking spot in the lease can stop that before it begins.

- Do you require the tenants to maintain a working fire alarm and CO detector? As property owners, we feel the need to ensure that the detectors remain installed and operational twice a year. However, the tenants do have the responsibility to not tamper with the units and inform us if they need repair.

- Have you got a clause dealing with the property's insurance or the tenant's content insurance? Insurance is by no means a sexy "purchase". Buying a video game or good book offers far more enjoyment. We all know that. But when bad things happen, the tenant needs to be aware that the landlord is not responsible for the tenant's contents, or finding them an alternative place to live. Also, as a property owner, there may be some restrictions to your insurance. Spelling out those restrictions in the lease can help in ensuring the insurance company doesn't use that provision as a reason to walk away from the claim.

- All good things must come to an end. Have you written out the rules for vacating the unit? Let it be known that you require a certain amount of notice, vacating requests to be on a certain document, and let them know that you will be allowed more regular access to the unit to show it to future renters. In provinces or states that allow for a rental security deposit, spell out the requirements to be able to get back that deposit in full.

- What is the deadline for when the exiting tenant must have everything moved out? Check with your state or province for guidance but write it down and remind them when they provide the notice. The next tenant may be ready to move in and such delays can cause a lot of hardship. Exiting tenants should also be reminded to return all house keys, mailbox keys, fobs, and garage door openers.

- It is smart to include a clause that deals with abandonment of a unit. After providing proper notice for entry, if you discover that the tenant's belongings are removed, and if the tenant has not paid you rent for that period, it constitutes abandonment of the unit. If there is some doubt, contact a local paralegal to discuss the matter.

If you don't deal with cannabis growth in the lease, does this mean you are permitting it in your building?

- Have you included a pet provision? Depending on your jurisdiction, it is difficult if not impossible to ban the entrance of the tenant's pets into the premises. Because of that, we insist on getting the tenant to acknowledge that they are responsible for any damage done by the animal. We even have the tenant sign a pet addendum schedule.

- Have you placed restrictions on smoking cigarettes or cannabis inside of the unit? This is a big deal for us. Growing cannabis in your unit is just nasty in many ways. Besides the excessive electricity consumption, there are also excessive humidity levels resulting from the activity which, in turn, can produce mold. Finally, there may be concerns about security at the leased premises, which is associated with the presence of cannabis growth. You may not be able to restrict tenants who smoke or take marijuana, but you can stop them from doing it inside the home.

- If the tenant "brings in" rodents, insects, or other vermin, it is at their cost to have them removed. If Dorothy from The Wizard of Oz had been a landlord, she would have likely been saying, Bed Bugs and Mice and Rats, oh my! If you are scratching your arm while thinking about this scenario, you are not alone. The more attentive you and/or your property manager is with the units, the less likely garbage will accumulate, which in turn keeps the rodent problem at bay.

- Did you ask for an emergency contact for the tenant? It is very important to have an emergency contact other than those living in the unit. If you really need to get into a unit or get in touch with a tenant who normally responds very quickly and you are concerned, then you should call this contact. Fire and emergency services may need their number as well. It also doesn't hurt to have an extra source to call in the event that the tenant vacates while still owing you money.

To anyone interested who has purchased this book, you can sign up on our website, www.ArmchairRealEstateMillionaire.com and receive our complete chapter of clauses, including my comments as to why we have prepared the clause. Keep in mind that some clauses may be a requirement in one market and banned in another. I always recommend that you do your due diligence before providing your lease for signing. We will also provide to you further addendums and checklists that you can use for yourself.

Our lease, or a portion of it, has now been used in hundreds of leases, mainly across Ontario. Some of the clauses are universal regardless of the region you live. We hope to reach out to our readers to provide us with leases they have had prepared to best protect them and their property. Feel free to pick and choose the clauses that can enhance the lease you already have, and send us recommendations of lease clauses that have worked in your market. We will be sure to provide you with an acknowledgment for your contribution.

But remember, no matter how rock solid your lease is, and no matter how much preparation you take in finding the property, renovating it to your liking, choosing the perfect tenant, or any other variable that you can think of, something WILL happen that you won't have expected. Your job as a long-term real estate investor is to deal with the problem at hand, and then adjust your policies and lease to try to prevent that thing from happening again.

Let's work together as a community to ensure the most thorough lease available.

"You can't have a million-dollar dream with a minimum wage work ethic."
—Stephen C. Hogan

ARMCHAIR MINDSET PLAYBOOK

🪑   The lease sets the tone for the relationship with your future tenant.

🪑   One day visiting a landlord / tenant board dispute hearing will show you the remarkable number of Landlord / tenant disputes arising from no initial lease or an illegal lease.

🪑   Go to the website http://www.ArmchairRealEstateMillionaire. com for lease clause examples.

CHAPTER 10

DON'T HANG YOUR HAT ON CAP RATES

*"It's impossible to live without failing at something, unless you
live so cautiously that you might as well have never lived at all,
in which case, you failed by default."*
—*J.K. Rowling*

When people assess the value of a property, they can use one
of two methods. The one most common in the residential
world is the comparison method and it goes a little something like this: If I own a three-bedroom home with two baths in a subdi-
vision, the first thing I should know is what other similar properties have
sold for in that area. From there, add or subtract based on key features
in the home. As you can imagine, this is a fair way to evaluate a residential home. If the last three similar homes sold for $500,000, $510,000,
and $515,000, there is a pretty good chance your property is also worth
$500,000–$515,000. Obviously, the condition of the home along with
other factors like time of year (in northern states and Canada cold weather months often reduce the number of buyers, thus affecting prices), location within the neighborhood (what street it's on, traffic flow, neighbors),
and the age of certain updates can sway the price point a bit, but using
comparables is a time-tested method of determining a property's value.

The second method of determining value is based on the revenue the property delivers. This is calculated using CAP rates. The **CAP**, or **Capitalization rate**, is defined as the ratio between the net operating income produced by an asset and its capital cost or alternatively its current market value. The rate calculated in a simple fashion is as follows:

CAP rate=annual net operating income/cost (or value).

For example, if a building is purchased for $1,000,000 and produces $60,000 in positive net operating income (the amount left over after the fixed and variable costs) during one year, then $60,000/$1,000,000=0.06 or 6 percent.

It's important to note that the cost associated with financing is NOT included in the net operating income (NOI) in determining CAP rates. Your first reaction might be that the cost of financing is a very important thing to consider and therefore should be included, but you would be confusing cash flow and return on investment (ROI) with the NOI.

Let me explain it in another way: two identical buildings are sitting right next to each other. Same neighborhood. Same age. Same condition. Let's even say the same rental income and expenses. The only difference between the two buildings is that building "A" is owned by the property owner "free and clear," meaning there is no mortgage or debt owned on the property. Meanwhile in building "B," the owner has a mortgage debt of $500,000. Let's now say that both properties are put up for sale. Just because property B has debt on it, that in itself should have no bearing on the purchase price to the new building's owner.

The idea behind creating a CAP rate is to compare one building to another based on the income it generates. It also allows someone to compare the real estate sector with equities and other investments.

CAP Rate Chart		Example
Revenue:	Rental Income	$100,000
Expenses:	Insurance	
	Municipal Tax	
	Property Management	
	Maintenance	
	Grass Cutting and Snow Removal	
	Vacancy Allowance	
	Garbage/Waste	$40,000
Net Operating Income (less financing)		$60,000
Accepted market CAP rate		5.0 percent
Property Value Calculation	NOI / CAP	$60,000 / .05
Market Value of the Property		$1,200,000

Chart 4A: CAP Rate Chart

Using this model, it's pretty easy to determine if a non-essential repair or renovation is worth the expense. If the repair or renovation can lead to higher rents without adding to the annual expenses, the renovation may be worth it.

Let's say the renovation will cost you $10,000 but will lead to an increase in monthly rent in one of the units of $200 a month. Is it worth it to do the work or re-rent it for the same rent you were receiving from the previous tenant? On the one hand, it will take you 50 months, or more than four years, to generate the extra $10,000 in revenue, which is a long time to wait. But what does it do to the property value? Continuing with the earlier example:

Original Net Operating Income (less financing)	$60,000
Added income ($200 per month)	$2,400
New Net Operating Income after renovation	$62,400
Accepted market CAP rate	5.0 percent

Property Value Calculation NOI / CAP	$62,400 / .05
New Market Value of the Property	$1,248,000

Chart 4B: Cap Rate

The $10,000 renovation, which brings in an additional $200 a month in rent, actually raises the value of the property by $48,000. Therefore, it is absolutely a smart decision to do that renovation. Remember, that is not even considering that you might attract better QUALITY TENANTS if renovation gives you a better showing, aka, a QUALITY PROPERTY.

In markets that have rent control limitations in which the rent can only rise 1–2 percent annually, I am often asked, "Is it worth it to go through the hassle of giving notice of a rent increase, piss off your existing tenants, and risk losing them?" The fact is that expenses are always rising. If you don't find ways to increase your revenue, the added expenses will actually reduce your NOI. That lower NOI can lower the value of that property. Plus, the goal of putting in all this effort is to turn a profit, ideally increasing that profit over time. My advice would be that if you can find a way to increase the NOI, you should try to take advantage of it. As little as $10 a month in extra NOI can really make a difference to the value of a building.

Monthly Increase in NOI	$10 (a month)	
Annual increase in NOI	$120	
5 percent CAP	$120 / .05	$2,400
6 percent CAP	$120 / .06	$2,000

Chart 4C: Cap Rate

Just $10 a month in rental income can instantly raise the value of the building by $2,000 on a 6 percent CAP. If you can find a way to increase the NOI by $50, which is very possible to do by just raising your rents when you are legally allowed to do so, you will raise the value of the building by $10,000 at a 6 percent CAP.

So now that you understand CAP and how it determines values, you're probably thinking, "This sounds great! It makes sense! Why on earth would Dominguez title the chapter to NOT hang your hat on CAP rates, besides the cute play on words?"

CAP RATE CHALLENGES

1. There is no true directory of accepted CAP rates in any market. Yes, experts and insiders can have a pretty good idea of the revenues and expenses of a particular building and can extrapolate an approximate CAP, but because most buildings are bought and sold by privately owned companies and individual land owners, the numbers are not officially disclosed. If I am an insider in a particular market and investment type, I might be able to estimate a CAP, then use that CAP to estimate the next property that becomes available.

2. Caveat Emptor is a Latin term roughly translated to mean Buyer Beware. That can certainly apply to a property's NOI statement. Most often, the statement the buyer sees is an estimate prepared by the seller or the seller's representative. SHOCKINGLY, the estimate is very favorable to the seller.

All it needs is a few cosmetic improvements

- This NOI presented to potential buyers is not audited, nor may it even bear any similarity to the actual results the seller delivered in the previous year.

- Typically, the rental income received will be the cumulation of each month's rent for each unit, assuming they were all filled for every moment of the year. One of the units may have been vacant for three-plus months, but that is rarely shown in the rent roll or NOI projection.

- The expenses may also be light. Even though the seller used a property manager, it is nowhere to be seen on the NOI projection. Nor is vacancy allowance, because according to the seller, there has NEVER been a vacancy in the unit. Why should they provide a vacancy allowance? Also, the repairs, maintenance, grass cutting, snow removal, and waste management are either absent from the projection or show ridiculously low projections going forward.

As you can imagine, as they say in the IT world, "garbage in, garbage out" (GIGO)—if revenue and expenses are not entirely accurate, when one multiplies the figure with the regional CAP rate, it will artificially raise the market value of the property. As a buyer, you need to analyze the data provided to you by the sellers or their representatives. Leases or statements of tenancy can give you a pretty decent idea of the ACTUAL rental income within the building. If a unit is vacant, your insider knowledge will give you a handle on the rents you can receive in its current state.

A mistake buyers and sellers often make when assessing value is to say, "OK, Mr. Buyer, if you do this renovation or evict this tenant, the income will be much better." That may be true or not true, but it just doesn't matter. When assessing the current value of a business or building or whatever, all you can base it on are the numbers of that business RIGHT NOW. If you feel you can run things better than the previous owner, then that is "future value." If you improve the business or property, then you benefit by raising the value. Conversely, if on your watch, the business or building has a decrease in

NOI, then the value goes down. People try to overcomplicate assessing the value of a business or building, but unless there is some unusual event in the building, like an expanded unit with another bedroom or perhaps an additional unit was created, the value doesn't just magically go up just because the seller wants it to.

I have an expression I like to share with my investors in a bigger city market that is desirable for investment: "If you show me a reported building with a 10 percent CAP rate, I'll show you a person who is lying about their building's NOI." So often, real estate salespeople come in and make outrageous profit claims; meanwhile so many of their expenses are simply omitted. I always think that if a business or individual were generating a 10 percent CAP, why in the world would they sell it?

3. Industry insiders study the market and analyze the property to determine the property's accurate market value. Amateur investors speculate on the market and the property and GAMBLE their wealth on a bet that everything will work out.

Amateur investors using the comparison method overpay for some properties. Because real estate values have experienced an unbelievable growth in my markets over the past decade, people have a lot of equity in their homes. Residents or homeowners take MAYBE one course on real estate investing, hear about it from a colleague or friend, or watch HGTV. They feel that they are now experts and real estate will be the key to their fortunes. Unfortunately, because they have no idea how to value a property and they likely work with the Realtor that helped them buy their family home maybe 10 years ago, they can't interpret the numbers correctly. They may have seen that a comparable property sold for a certain price, but don't realise it was totally renovated, had no deferred maintenance issues, and was receiving market-leading rent. The subject property they are considering doesn't compare well at all. But the amateur investor buys the property anyway because they speculate that real estate values ALWAYS go up.

CHOOSING REAL ESTATE AS YOUR INVESTMENT SAFE HAVEN

As it becomes more and more difficult to find safe investment vehicles out there, investors are gravitating to real estate. Throughout the past five-plus years, investors across most major North American markets are willing to purchase a property that has a much lower CAP rate than they would have been willing to do pre–Great Recession, or even during the peak of the recession.

For example, in Toronto, where once 6 percent was the low number, now I'm seeing deals transpire at rates under 4 percent. Even in Oshawa, a city 40 kilometers east of Toronto, and where I own much of my real estate portfolio, where once 8 percent was acceptable, I've seen a couple of deals in the past few months sell for well under 5 percent. Capitalization rates are a calculation of the yield of the investment, and an indirect measure of how fast an investment will pay for itself. For a property with a CAP rate of 10 percent the payback is 10 years. At 6 percent, it is 16.6 years.

If you have been investing in equities for more than a few years, you likely have experienced multiple corrections in the market. If you're like most people, you're probably squeamish about parking all your money in equity markets and hoping for the best.

It's because of the perceived reputation of real estate as a "safe haven" that CAP rates are declining. It's that flood of new investors entering the real estate investment market that is creating the competition and leading to those lower CAP rates.

"So what?" you say. "That only comes into play when I sell the property." Not always true, I answer. Once you have built enough equity in the building, you can do a bank refinance and get much of your initial investment and/or renovation costs out of the property while still maintaining a debt-to-equity ratio that our very conservative banks will accept. The other, more difficult to measure benefit of doing the reno, is that you can attract a more desirable tenant. And there are a lot of benefits to having a good tenant.

__Insider Tip:__ You can earn tax-free money through real estate investing. If you can build the equity in the property to a point where a lender is willing to loan you a higher amount than what you already owe (refinance), then you are receiving this money tax free. Sophisticated investors use this method to recycle their available funds to obtain more properties and grow their portfolio.

INVESTING IN A TERTIARY MARKET

One of my clients owned a property in a small, rural town about two hours east of Toronto. The building was originally a school but was converted into a 12-unit building in the 1980s. Because she was singularly focused on cash flow and an awesome CAP rate, this property made sense to purchase. On paper, the cash flow numbers were remarkable. The challenge came in the ongoing management of the property. The previous owner did not update any of the units and had a lot of deferred maintenance issues. When my client bought it, she began work right away on improving the units. The property was over three hours away from where she lived, so organizing property management, renovations, and general handyman work proved difficult. To make matters more complicated, even finding local workers proved challenging.

But I thought that real estate values ALWAYS goes up!

Because there was little local employment, the vacancy rate remained higher than expected. Those that did apply were often on some form of social assistance. Many of these tenants either did not care for the unit or did not always pay rent.

On paper, this property was a home run IF all the units were rented, the tenants were paying rent on time, and repairs were minimal. Only then would the property have incredible cash flow numbers. However, after four years, that never once happened.

Eventually, my client grew tired of the long commute to check in on the property and maintain it and after she added up the numbers, made the decision to sell. Because it was in such an undesirable market, the value hadn't changed that much. Had she purchased a boring bungalow with a basement apartment in a primary or even secondary market, meaning a property located in a growing market that contains great or even good market fundamentals, investors would have been lining up to pay her close to double what she had paid for it.

After months of effort, the property was sold and our client ended her run as a real estate investor. Although she did make a little on the overall transaction, the effort she had put into it, along with the hardship of managing it discouraged her to try again.

I hope that the experience didn't "break" her ambition to build generational wealth. Too many people leave the industry not because it's ineffective, but because of a bad experience. Often the novice investor simple buys the wrong property or selects the wrong tenant. A couple of bad decisions really can make you want to quit the business.

IF NOT CAP, THEN WHAT?

So, you might be wondering, if CAP rates are that easily manipulated, what are the things I should be looking at when determining whether a property is a good investment or not? The two things I track more than anything else are cash flow and ROI. We have discussed each of these methods of tracking a property in previous chapters, however it's worth repeating that it's never a good idea to buy into negative cash flow. The expected rental income must at minimum, meet or hopefully exceed the expected ongoing expenses, including financing costs.

It can help to analyze what you REALLY WANT. If you have a solid nine-to-five job making enough income to support your lifestyle, then it's likely ROI is the most important number to chart. If you have no other income source, and no way to put bread on the table, then focus on cash flow.

As I mentioned in Chapter 4, Leveraging Your Way into the Triple Crown Club, my immediate goal to this point has been ROI. I have a limited amount of funds available to me and need to recycle those funds over and over. I do that by refinancing my existing portfolio and taking out available equity as a means of using those re-acquired funds to reinvest into another property. Each time I refinance my properties, my debts go up on it, thus increasing that property's expenses and decreasing its cash flow. However, if much of my invested money is returned to me, my remaining equity in the property will experience a substantial ROI.

If you have invested $120,000 into a property and the mortgage paydown and appreciation is approximately $30,000, the ROI is 25 percent for the year. Whereas if you have invested just $60,000 into that property, the mortgage paydown and appreciation won't change. It remains at around $30,000. But because the lower amount of your money within that investment remains, the ROI would be 50 percent. There are properties in our portfolio where ALL our initial investment has been removed—the ROI on a property with nothing invested into it is INFINITE.

That, my friends, is a pretty good return.

PUTTING A LID ON CAPS (COULDN'T HELP IT)

The next time you read a prospectus and see a listed CAP rate, you'll know what they mean. But a word of warning: the numbers may not be what they seem. I still use CAP as a tool when evaluating whether or not to do a renovation or nonessential repair and as I've said before, if there are no appropriate comparable properties, CAP can give you a reasonable estimate on a valuation. But if you ever see a listing where the seller or his agent lists a CAP that far exceeds the market CAP for your area, look closer at those numbers and the quality of the unit. You will likely find holes in both the prospectus and the building's foundation or repairs.

WHAT'S THE END GAME?

It is typically true that you can't keep refinancing the properties by releveraging them over and over forever. For one thing, obtaining traditional bank financing gets more and more difficult as your portfolio grows. Obviously, the more properties you own, the more issues you will often need to deal with. The good news is, because you have purchased QUALITY PROPERTIES in QUALITY NEIGHBORHOODS, your day-to-day work is minimal. But, either way, at some point, the size of the portfolio may become a hassle. Keep in mind that because your ROI is so strong, selling your property will slow the level of growth on your net worth. But if you want to change course and look to enhance your cash flow, these very same properties can start to deliver this to you.

Your largest expense on a monthly basis is your debt financing. With past refinancing efforts, that debt may even be greater than your initial purchase prices. But each property should have reasonable cash flow, especially if you are willing to stop growing the portfolio and simply HOLD that portfolio for five or more years. But now is the time to start earning the cash flow!

If you have amassed a portfolio of four properties, you can now look to sell two of those buildings. Because of mortgage paydown and appreciation, the equity in the property may just be enough to pay off a property you choose to maintain. There will be tax implications, of course, but if you can wind up with two free and clear properties, your cash flow per property will be enormous. If you were able to get up to six properties, look to keep three. With 10 properties you may wind up with four or five, ALL OWNED FREE AND CLEAR.

That should be awfully effective in delivering the cash flow revenue you desire in order to live your best life.

Your remaining properties will deliver "fruit" every month as long as you live, if that is what you want. You can hire a quality property manager and still generate consistent income for as long as you have your portfolio. But the "tree" that generated the fruit can also be your legacy for your heirs. They can choose to sell the properties and take the cash, or keep collecting the fruit for the duration of their lifetime. That "cash for life" gift can help future generations in your own family tree.

Or maybe you just keep your portfolio intact, and then as revenues rise and debt falls, cash flow and net wealth will continue to grow. Depending on your needs, it's nice to have options.

"Money frees you from doing things you dislike. Since I dislike doing nearly everything, money is handy."
—Groucho Marx

SUCCESS STORY
Anita Bongers-Lewis and Kris Lewis

This dynamic duo, at the time in their mid-30s, had already made some progress long before we met. Kris and Anita had purchased two preconstruction condos as investments, an additional condo Kris owned before they met, and their "forever" home in the suburbs, all while each making solid six-figure incomes.

By most people's standards, they were getting ahead. But they were looking for more. They wanted to build enough wealth to take them "away from the working world as well as create exponential wealth," and they were looking for an investment vehicle that would allow them to do that.

Being super analytical, they had a spreadsheet that showed them where they were and how long it would take for them to reach their goals at their current pace. Their current plan was simply taking them too long to get them to where they wanted to be. They didn't want to wait until the average person was able to retire; they wanted to reach their goals faster.

They read books, listened to podcasts, and read a lot of articles on an assortment of wealth building subjects. It was while accumulating that knowledge that Kris heard a podcast where I spoke about wealth building in real estate.

The podcast resonated with Kris and he took action to reach out and chat real estate with me. After that, they hired a coach and began attending local investment group meet-ups. They were committed to learning all they could about real estate. Once they decided on their course of action, nothing was going to stop them from reaching their goals.

They were initially hesitant as no one in their family had ever purchased rental investment properties. As Kris says, friends and family "didn't understand what we understood to be the truth about real estate, and there were a lot of people skeptical. But no one said we shouldn't be doing it or anything like that."

They were initially nervous about being taken advantage of because they heard about the $20,000 real estate courses and didn't really have a relationship with anyone in the industry. They liked what they were learning from the Doors to Wealth team, but they still wanted to verify this information with other sources.

One of the things they enjoyed early on was the ability to network with other more established investors and ask them questions and learn about some of their challenges. Attending local meet-ups and our Realtor investor tours gave them that chance to verify with others the legitimacy of real estate investing. Seeing the properties on the tour for themselves allowed them to take what they were learning in theory and see what they could do with that knowledge. It made it real for them. They realised they could do it.

They admit there have been some challenges along the way. Some projects took way longer than they were expecting; challenges with the city in the legalization process, tenant challenges, and more. But nothing has ever come up so severe that ever made them consider selling their portfolio and doing something else.

This power couple has been doing real estate investing for about five years now and today owns eight investment properties (including the FIVE they bought in their first year of action-taking). They dedicate about 10 hours most months on their portfolio, dealing with tenants and solving minor issues.

The decision to invest in real estate didn't just help their net worth. "It's not the wealth, it's the difference between retiring at 65 and retiring at 45. It's living the life that you want to live and that's by design. It's hanging out with people who think like you." They say that they don't use any of the money from their real estate right now, as they don't need to; it will afford them the future they want eventually, but it's there now if they had an emergency.

Over the years they have been more focused on wealth-building over cash flow. Any cash flow that they have earned to this point has gone back into future down payments. They have been able to refinance some of their first purchases and again used those funds for future down payments. They sold their initial dream home and used some of those funds for purchasing new properties. Both Anita and Kris know they have plenty of time to purchase a big home again, but their goals changed, and their "dream home" was no longer part of those goals.

Anita stresses how important it was to work with a team early on "that practices what they preach. People that are actually in it and doing it and advising you based on experience and not based on a book that anyone could read." She appreciated the process and developing real relationships.

She felt strongly enough about helping others reach their goals that she went out and got her real estate license and immediately joined the Doors to Wealth Real Estate Group. "Retirement" from her initial six-figure income as a chiropractor may not be what she initially thought it would look like, but being a Realtor has allowed her to re-focus on their portfolio, afforded her more time with her family, and of course offered opportunities to network and help others get involved in real estate investing.

Kris stresses that he couldn't have imagined how that initial conversation would change their lives as much as it did. They were doing the "big home in the suburbs" plan with little hope of getting to where they wanted when they wanted. Although it may have started with one podcast, leading to one phone call, then one meeting, it was the fact that Kris and Anita chose to take action, and then after doing so, doing it again and again. Both Anita and Kris admit to now being seminar and meet-up junkies, but today they share their experiences and challenges with others who are just starting and looking to follow a similar path to success and wealth.

ARMCHAIR MINDSET PLAYBOOK

🕊️ CAP rate is the calculation of the annual net operating income divided by the cost or value of the asset.

🕊️ Always be cautious of CAP rates provided by the seller or their representatives. Verify the numbers to ensure that all expenses are covered and the income generated is accurate and not some unrealistic projection.

🕊️ Industry insiders study the market and analyze the property to determine the property's accurate market value.

🕊️ "Tax free money" through real estate is possible by re-financing an asset you own that has accrued significant equity.

🕊️ When an investor is able to get back their entire initial investment from the purchase of an investment, the ROI going forward is an infinite percentage.

CHAPTER 11

A PART-TIME JOB THAT WILL MAKE YOU A MILLIONAIRE

"You never know who's swimming naked until the tide goes out."
—Warren Buffett

Because investors don't work in their properties on a daily basis, like restaurant or retail store staff do, most tax laws regard income generated from the owning of real estate investments as "passive income."

Let me explain first what **"passive income"** means. One definition is, "Income resulting from cash flow received on a regular basis, requiring minimal to no effort by the recipient to maintain it."[23]

A passive income investment does NOT mean a totally hands-off investment that requires little to no thought after the investment is made.

Admittedly, you aren't expected to show up at the property at 9 a.m. to punch a time clock. There is no area foreman or supervisor checking in to see if you did your work on time and to a good standard. However, you have an asset (or series of assets) with value. Your tenants are clients who pay you money every month. You have expenses to pay, regardless of what kind of revenue you receive. You may have heard the expression, "If it walks like a duck, and quacks like a duck, then it is a duck." Owning a property has assets like a business, liabilities like a business, and clients like a business, therefore it is a business.

The reason why I press the issue to treat it like a business is simply because so many property owners miss that very important step. They don't treat their investment seriously and they fail in the most important rules of business management: their investment doesn't see positive cash flow revenue; they defer needed maintenance and repairs; they don't spend enough time seeking a good tenant (client); and they go into the investment gambling that the value will go up, with few to no exit strategies if that doesn't happen.

Have you ever driven past a store or restaurant and said to yourself, "I wonder how long they will stay in business?" Maybe the product they offer doesn't fit in with the neighborhood or perhaps has little chance to generate the revenue needed to survive long-term. Sure enough, more often than not, six months to one year later the business has shut down.

The great news about residential real estate is that it offers a MUCH higher percentage of success than a retail store or a restaurant. You do not need to be an expert in the field to get started in this business. We have discussed in great detail the importance of buying correctly. We have also discussed the benefits of holding on to the asset long-term, and the potential windfall that can come from doing so.

But what about those boring years in between buying the property and the eventual refinance or sale of the units? They are important. In fact, it's the details in those "boring years" of holding the assets that can in fact make you wealthy and successful in this business.

Here is a list of ongoing "jobs" that every property owner should complete, even if they are not doing it themselves, to better their chances at success.

SIX-MONTH INSPECTIONS/MAINTENANCE VISITS

Many novice real estate investors place all responsibility for the maintenance of their rental units on the tenants themselves. While it's true that many responsible tenants will maintain the unit, it's unlikely they will give it the same level of care as we would, as property owners.

There is no question that reviewing the properties is a pain in the ass. It's far easier to NOT visit the units. Put it off for another month... However, if you don't keep an eye on things, you might not know if there are problems that need your attention.

In the six-month inspection, we do the following:

1. **Replace the furnace filter.**

   We maintain a master list of each furnace we own, and the size of the filter required. Because filters don't go bad, if they're ever on sale we stock up on them. You can tell the tenants to replace the filters and can even have it in their lease to do so, but if they don't, the worst that will happen to them is less air circulation and perhaps less heat or air conditioning. But for us, a clogged filter can cause the furnace to overwork, which shortens its life, costing you big bucks. If there are pets in the house, ensure that the tenant has a supply of filters and remind them when it's time to replace it.

2. **Test carbon monoxide and smoke detectors.** Here's a simple form (but that's a good thing, as you'll be more likely to do it).

UNIT CARBON MONOXIDE AND SMOKE DETECTOR TEST

Date: _____

Address: _____

Unit: _____

Carbon Monoxide detector and smoke detector has been tested as a result of:

REASON: MOVE IN TO UNIT / MAINTENANCE

A) Carbon monoxide and smoke detector is securely fastened to the wall or ceiling

      YES   NO

B) Carbon monoxide and smoke detector shows no evidence of physical damage, paint application, or excessive grease and dirt accumulations

      YES   NO

C) Ventilation holes on the carbon monoxide and smoke detectors are clean and free of obstructions

      YES   NO

D) Carbon monoxide and smoke detector signal sounds when the test device is operated

      YES   NO

E) If battery operated, batteries have been replaced on _____

        YES   NO

LANDLORD NAME: _____

SIGNATURE: _____

TENANT NAME: _____

SIGNATURE: _____

6. **Do a quick visual inspection of the exterior of the unit.** We do a quick walk around the building to check for:

A) Debris around the yard, abandoned vehicles, clutter, etc. We don't want our place becoming a junkyard—for our benefit, the tenant's safety, and our property's neighbors.

B) Damage to the roof and shingles and any repairs required.

C) Blockages from leaves or branches in the eves and downspout, making sure they remain connected properly.

D) Any damage to fences, noting their condition.

E) Cracks and potholes in the driveway.

F) Potential problems with trees in the yard to see if there is any cause for alarm for the trees themselves or the building.

G) Rodent infestation, damage, or maintenance issues in the shed, garage, or outbuilding. We also peek inside the shed to make sure that the tenants are not using it to store rotting garbage.

    When it comes to maintenance of rental buildings, water is the enemy. From the attic to the foundation to the plumbing in the home, reviewing them regularly helps to safeguard you and your investments from very costly repairs.

8. **Do a quick visual inspection of the inside of the unit.** Watch for hoarder tendencies, damage from pets, moisture concerns, smells from smoking in the unit, and any sign of the use or manufacture of drugs.

I consider myself a master delegator. If there are jobs I don't want to do, I hire others to do them on my behalf. At our house, regular "chores" such as housecleaning, lawn cutting, snow shovelling, swimming pool cleaning and maintenance, and an assortment of handyman tasks have been delegated away from us. This has freed us up to spend more time on our business or simply to enjoy life. It took me years to learn that although I really like living in a clean house, I got no pleasure out of doing the actual house cleaning. The same was true with a freshly cut lawn; I never loved going out there and actually cutting it myself. So, we delegated it to others.

When it comes to doing a visual inspection of your rental units, this is one thing that should NOT be delegated, unless it's to a trusted, experienced property manager.

Entering the unit to change a battery in a smoke detector seems too simple a job and a waste of your valuable time. Perhaps it is. But the REAL immediate reason for the walk-through is to make sure nothing weird is happening in your properties.

Because you properly screened your tenants and you have attracted QUALITY TENANTS, this is perhaps a remote possibility, but things can happen over time. Perhaps the tenant has a new boyfriend who is into some illegal activity. Perhaps the tenant chooses to bring in a litter of dogs or cats. Perhaps the tenant begins to let the place fall apart and to hoard all sorts of garbage.

Just because they pay their rent on the first day of every month does not mean that there are no issues happening in your place. A quick visual inspection can nip a potential problem in the bud.

We even tell potential new tenants about our diligence and regular checks. Good tenants are appreciative of these efforts and take comfort in knowing that the property owners take pride in their rental units. It is my hope that by saying we will be doing regular checks, we will discourage potential "bad tenants" from choosing our place to rent. They would rather pick a property where they will not be visited by the owner.

CASE STUDY
INSURANCE DOESN'T COVER DAMAGE FROM ILLEGAL ACTIVITY

As a property owner, you want to do everything properly. You should get full insurance to protect you in the event of disaster. It might be worth checking in with your insurance broker to see how the coverage would work if, say, a tenant blew up the building during the manufacture of illegal narcotics. Let's say the tenant creates his own personal meth lab and something goes wrong and the resulting explosion and fire effectively destroys the building.

Most, if not all, insurance policies have disclaimer riders stating that if the damage came as a result of illegal activity, the claim will not be honored. As the property owner, you will still have the mortgage payments with the lender, but no home or rental income to support those payments. To make matters worse, once your lender learns that the home is no longer occupiable, they can "call the mortgage" which means the borrower either needs to pay it off or find another lender willing to loan out the funds.

Whether the home is a single-family dwelling, contains two or three units, or is a multiunit apartment building, the insurance rules remain the same on damages resulting from illegal activity.

We have been fortunate that none of our, nor any of our clients' properties have ever had a meth lab or grow operation inside any of their units, however, I can share that the landlords who are diligent in their student rentals have a far different experience than those property owners who let the kids run wild.

9. **Ensure the keys we have "on file" work properly and the tenants haven't changed the locks.**

We maintain a locked cabinet of all keys for each of our properties. They are marked nice and clear in case we need them in a hurry. It's pretty rare that we have had this issue, but there have been times when a tenant has changed the lock of the unit without notifying us. Usually it was because a girlfriend or boyfriend moved out and they wanted to ensure that their ex had no further access. In this situation we explained that they violated the lease agreement and if they required a lock change, they should have let us know. We checked that the lock was changed properly, then got a working key cut for our files and instructed them to not do it again. Had we not checked the locks with our existing keys, we never would have known about the lock change.

10. **Verify the contact information you have for each tenant is correct and try to get emergency contact information for each tenant.**

In our experience, tenants are very friendly…until they're not. Although we have had many tenants leave on good terms and we would absolutely rent to them again, there are others that, perhaps because of the stress of the impending move, issues causing the move, or something else entirely, became hostile to work with. It's because of this that it's never a good idea to ask for emergency contact details at the end of the lease. If the tenant leaves crap behind, or unpaid rent or utility bills, they may not be that keen to hear from you. Getting their parents' number on file from the outset is a good idea if there are issues after the tenancy is completed.

We genuinely ask for emergency contact details in the event of an actual emergency. Tenants typically are most amenable to giving you this information at the beginning of the tenancy. However, in our experience, we have mostly used the contact information to locate the tenant for other more financial reasons after they leave.

11. **Do a quick visual inspection to see if there are obvious**

signs of additional people or pets in the unit that you are unaware of.

How would you know if your tenant has sublet the extra bedrooms to other people and you have a form of rooming house in your possession? How about if your tenant has a secret desire to be a zookeeper and is getting a great start at her goals by owning and housing three dogs, five cats, a rabbit, a snake, multiple rodents, two love birds, an ant farm, and a sea monkey exhibit?

That 10-minute visit spent changing the battery in the smoke detector or changing a furnace filter is looking better and better now, isn't it?

12. **Ask the tenant about any maintenance issues within the unit or on the property that require attention.**

It may surprise you to learn that the biggest issue with good tenants is they rarely, if ever, call you if there is a problem. Your first reaction might be: how is that a problem? But sometimes you want to hear from them. By asking the tenant while you are there, you can discover their maintenance concerns. They usually begin with: "I didn't want to bother you, but ..." Things like cracked window panes, leaky toilets or sinks, cracks in the tub surround, a little bit of mold in spots, and regular fuses blown can be signs of much bigger issues. Just like anyone else, I don't like spending money on repairs, but dealing with problems quickly can reduce the damage and the expense further down the line. If you don't ask the question, you may not get the information until it is a big deal!

13. **Read and take photo of the water meter.**

It's a little thing, but if you are responsible for paying the water bill (even if you're then reimbursed by the tenant) get into the habit of taking a photo of the number on the water meter. Tenants responsible for paying the utilities may not be entirely truthful about the number on the meter if that means their bill will be higher.

14. **(In the fall) Have any exterior hoses and taps shut off and put away. Put away the lawn mower.**

If your property is in an area that has regular freezing weather in the winter, it's vital that you shut off the exterior taps to ensure that the water doesn't freeze inside the tap, causing significant damage. It's also smart to make sure the hose, lawn mower, and other items you might provide to the tenants are safely put away for the winter months. A little prevention can extend the life of these items.

15. **Do an interior fire safety check.**

Proper fire prevention is the most important prevention you will have to deal with (other than water prevention, which is more common). It is just smart to make sure that everything is fine from a fire safety standpoint. When doing your walk-through inspection:

A) Ensure all fire doors are closed properly and the egress is clear. Make sure the self-closing mechanisms are working properly.

B) Inspect for overloaded circuits and a spider web of extension cords. Too many electronic items on one circuit can cause issues and lead to sparks or a fire.

C) Look for garbage around the furnace. Although the furnace's spark is designed to be contained, it simply isn't a good idea to have papers or flammable materials surrounding it.

D) Inspect dryer vents for lint and clean out regularly. Through regular use, lint can build up inside of the vent, which can form a blockage. At minimum, it can affect the effectiveness of the dryer and shorten the appliance's lifespan, but far worse, lint can start a fire.

E) Inspect receptacle plugs throughout the unit. Older plugs occasionally need to be replaced as they do wear out with use.

REPAIR WORK

The "old-school" approach to property management for some long-time investors was "a dollar saved is a dollar earned." Short term, that is absolutely correct. However, the net effect of avoiding obvious needed repairs will be further damage to the building, and, in the long term, will have an effect on the quality of tenants and the amount of rent the landlord can attract to the building.

If you recall the chapter on CAP rates we discussed the value of increasing rents in terms of the market value of the property. In short, it often makes sense to spend some money in repairing the property, especially when the repair can lead to a better tenant profile and better rents.

Not every repair is necessary. There will always be "nice to haves that we never get around to doing." When we come across a potential repair or restoration, we ask the following questions:

- Does not doing the repair cause further damage to the building?

- Does not doing the repair affect the enjoyment of the existing tenant or detract from attracting quality tenants in the future?

- Does not doing the repair affect potential future rent?

If the answer is NO in all instances, it might make sense to defer this repair to a later date, however, if the answer is YES to one or more of these questions, you should add this repair to the work schedule.

ANYTHING related to "water" or "mold" should be given the highest priority, as deferring these repairs will certainly build up problems over time and cost you way more in the end. If the water is coming up from the ground, the only solution may be a full foundation repair, but most often, water and mold prevention can be a moderate, very occasional expense. Here's a quick recap of Chapter 7, Don't Let Your Investment Go Underwater, and a checklist of things to consider when doing that visual inspection.

- Cleaning out the eavestroughs (in areas with lots of trees, this could be twice a year).

- Reattaching the downspouts (and adding in an extension) so that the water comes out at least 4 feet away from the house's foundation.

- Ensuring the venting out of the house, especially through the attic, is connected and functioning properly.

- Improving the grading all around the home, including soil and pavement where the driveway approaches the foundation. Remember water finds a way of settling at the lowest point, make sure that point isn't against your foundation.

- Cutting roots in the drain pipes. If you have big trees in the neighborhood, consider having a plumber throw a camera into your drainpipe to ensure that there are no blockages. Over time, roots find a way into the water from the drain, and when materials are flushed down the toilet, it can form a blockage. A partial blockage leads to a slow drain of the waste. A total blockage will lead to a sewage backup.

- Installing a washing machine drain pan or bladder under every machine. One day the machine will break down. When that happens, it may leak out of the machine. If that washing machine is located in the upper level of a two-unit home, that water will pour out and work its way into the lower unit, damaging everything it touches. Even if the pan isn't connected to a drain, just having it there to hold the water in the event of a leak can divert a catastrophe. Yeah it is an expense that will seem unnecessary, until the day happens when the unit breaks down.

Insider Tip: If there is a leak or flood in the unit, it's the property owner's responsibility to repair the issue and repair the unit, however, it is the TENANT's responsibility to replace their belongings or find alternative accommodation if the unit is uninhabitable. Continue to stress the importance of tenant insurance and even get the tenant to acknowledge that they are aware that the property owner is not responsible for replacement of personal belongings in the unit in the event of flooding or water damage.

TENANT DISPUTES AND DEALING WITH NONPAYMENT OF RENT

The fear of dealing with unruly tenants and overall tenant disputes is undoubtedly the number one thing holding most potential investors back from taking action and buying an investment property.

One of the most common questions I get is, "If I have two tenants essentially in the same house, won't they have disputes with each other?" The answer, if you have properly renovated and designed your building is, "A lot less than you might think."

By building your investment with little to no common area, the chances of tenant disputes are reduced. Combine that with proper soundproofing and proper tenant selection and you will find the complaints are minimal.

When possible, we separate the laundry, each tenant has their own driveway lane, and sometimes we have even offered each tenant their own private, fenced, back yard space.

That said, when a complaint does occur, as property owner, you need to take it seriously. This is their home and it's your responsibility to ensure their safe enjoyment of the place.

We find that most complaints fall under the following categories:

HE SAID/SHE SAID

These are typically the most common complaints. "Can you believe that Susie did this?" "Did you hear what Johnny did in the upper unit the other day?" In these situations, we hear out the tenant, then ask if they want us to speak with the other tenant about the situation. Sometimes a quick call can alleviate ongoing issues.

If the problem is big enough to affect one tenant's enjoyment of the occupancy, then we ask them to issue us a written complaint with time, date, and specifics. This letter goes into the file and if the behavior doesn't change, may lead to us terminating the tenancy at some point.

VIOLATION OF THE LEASE

Issues like smoking in the unit, excessive noise, bringing in an appliance without notifying the owner, excessive junk abandoned in the yard, and leaving rotting garbage in a shed attracting rodents are all things that we have accounted for in the lease and can follow up with a notice either to repair, or to cease doing what they are doing.

Again, if necessary, we ask the complaining tenant to keep a record of when and where the incident occurred as, chances are, we won't be near the unit to confront the accused tenant when they pull out that cigarette.

The first time a tenant violates the lease there is a temptation to just give them a verbal warning and hope that the situation corrects itself. But let me share that every nightmare-like tenant had a first incident in their tenancy, then a second, and so forth. When it comes to evicting a problem tenant, "verbal warnings" tend to be ignored by a judge or adjudicator. Start the file with the first complaint serious enough to take action on. Hopefully, this incident is the first and only complaint worth issuing a written warning for. But if it is not, you will be very happy that you started the file immediately.

VIOLENCE OR CRIMINAL ACTIVITY

In the rare event that you receive a call from one tenant about some illegal activity, your immediate response must be for them to contact the police or 911. We have been fortunate to not have this happen very often.

CASE STUDY.
GET OUT OF MY LIFE!

The longer you are a real estate investor, the more likely it is that you'll encounter a tenant you don't get along with. Maybe they're the type to complain about everything. They don't get along with their co-tenant neighbor. They might have been partially responsible for one or more tenants moving out, as the responsible tenant couldn't deal with their craziness. Even if the tenant hasn't fallen behind on their rent, they seem to be causing you more time and headaches than everyone else combined.

We recently had this situation and Lisa even considered selling the property just to get rid of this person. We decided that life is too short. Over the years, the police had been called to that unit multiple times (the only two-unit property in our portfolio where this has happened). The tenant would complain about EVERYTHING. She was sneaky. It turned out she had some mental health issues that she chose not to medicate. Nothing dangerous, but she was a nuisance and created undue stress to her neighbors and us as property owners. This person needed to go.

The cool thing about building some wealth in this industry is that you have a little flexibility to buy yourself out of problems. This tenant wasn't a happy person. She wasn't happy in our unit. We decided to make her a one-time offer to get her out—we'd cover the equivalent of four months' rent and pay for her moving expenses. In most markets, you might think we went overboard. In a market like San Francisco, a property owner might laugh and say, "That's it?" But in total we compensated her with about $8,000 to get the hell out of our life.

It wasn't a case of wanting more rent, although we chose to renovate the unit after she left with the intention of charging the next tenant a few bucks more. It was simply a case of not wanting to deal with that person anymore. As a parting gift, as she left, she turned off the heat (in the middle of winter). We had to go to the property that night to turn the heat back on so the downstairs tenant could have some warmth. GOOD RIDDANCE!

Any cases of domestic violence, breaking and entering, assault, sale of narcotics, and more are all illegal activities and the authorities should be the first to deal with these complaints. As property owner, documenting the incident and adding it to the file is the next step. Only then can the owner file for an eviction.

NONPAYMENT OR LATE PAYMENT OF RENT

As a property owner, you have bills to pay. EVERY month you are responsible for the mortgage, taxes, insurance, and in many cases, the utilities. As a responsible property owner, you can't tell your creditors that you won't pay them until you get paid by the tenant. They will not be understanding. Receiving your rental income on time keeps the process moving along. When that doesn't happen, you need to find other means to pay the bills.

It's my experience that any tenant neglecting his rent payment makes the choice to not pay that bill, because it has the least consequence. Failure to pay for their car loan, cell phone, or cable bill can result in an immediate loss of service of something they value. They don't hold their landlord in the same regard as the cell phone company, in large part, because of the lack of consequence.

In many provinces and states, you can't simply evict a tenant for a couple of late payments, but by "papering the file" you are building a case for future eviction. By doing so, the tenant learns that you are serious about wanting your rent on time. They will (hopefully) then rank "paying for housing" higher on their priority list.

Become familiar with the proper, accepted paperwork in your province or state that can be used to start the eviction process for lack of rental payment. Showing up with your bank statement and pointing to the days on which rent was actually deposited will not likely be recognized by the court as evidence and is not grounds for you to kick out the negligent tenant.

Never, ever, EVER give the tenant a break for a week or month on paying rent. You have bills to pay. If the rent is due on the first of the month and the tenant can't pay you until the 15th, what confidence do you have that he'll be able to pay you on the first of the next month?

You hear the horror story of the landlord who lost 6 to 12 months' rent because of nonpayment. In this situation, I place a lot of blame directly on the property owner. When the money doesn't arrive on the first of the month, the tenant should receive notification of late rent on the second or third of the month. Simple. Follow the process as offered by the state or province and get that eviction or settlement.

Before I scare you too much, if you have done your diligence during the application process, and you have selected what you feel is a QUALITY TENANT, then the risk is greatly reduced that you will have a frequently late rent-payer.

BOOKKEEPING AND PREPARATION FOR TAXES

When you read this heading, about 5 percent of you will let out a smile or a quick cheer, as you likely derive some sick, perverse pleasure out of maintaining your paperwork. For the remaining 95 percent of us, the sound was more of a grumble or perhaps some form of expletive. However, there are ways to GREATLY reduce the amount of time and stress this work will take in your life.

- Have separate bank accounts. If you run a business, it makes sense to have a separate bank account for that business. The same holds true for owning an investment property. By using that account for all money going in and all money going out, you have already separated your transactions for use later on. Even if you use a debit card for a transaction, ensure that the money comes directly from the account for that property. It may mean having multiple debit cards in your wallet, but the time saving on the back end is huge.

Insider Tip: If you own multiple properties, bite the bullet and open multiple bank accounts. There is often a small monthly charge for having extra accounts, however, the time savings or reduced bookkeeper fees should more than make up for it. If you decide to grow your portfolio, and possibly take on partners, separate bank accounts will become mandatory. Creating a strong business practice foundation while you are small can allow you to expand and manage your real estate investment business, or your small business, more effectively.

- Get a business credit card. It does not need to be a corporate card with expensive annual dues, just one that you only use for business-related expenses. Again, the purpose is to separate these expenses from your personal expenses.

- Keep your receipts. Always. I used to be guilty of not keeping my receipts. It's a pain to remember to save all those pieces of paper. But a bookkeeper once told me that if she gave me a $50 bill, would I also not take care of that? She said to think of the receipts as money, because without them you are essentially giving up money. There are a ton of different ways out there to "file" and load your business receipts. Some people take a photo of each receipt and have an app that keeps them together; some put everything in their wallet and write down the reason for keeping the receipt right on it; and some simply put everything in a shoe box and let someone else deal with it. I know of one person who created an email account specifically for their bookkeeping paperwork, and every time they received an emailed receipt, forwarded it to that address. It doesn't matter what your system is, just make sure you have one. You wouldn't catch Microsoft or Apple telling their shareholders that, "We think we're doing well, but bookkeeping is a pain, and no one wanted to do it this year."

The benefit of staying on top of your bookkeeping is that you can calculate your profit and loss (P&L) statement and cash flow analysis for each property. Your P&L statement is a way of keeping score of how your business is doing.

You don't need to overthink this P&L statement. It can be really simple.

Earnings: Rent Received _____

Other Income _____

Total Earnings: _____

Expenses: Mortgage Interest _____

Property Insurance _____

Property Taxes _____

Utilities (paid by owner) _____

Repairs and Maintenance _____

Bank Charges _____

Other Miscellaneous Expenses _____

Total Expenses: _____

Gross Profit (or loss): _____

Notes:

A) The mortgage payment is typically made up of both interest and principal. For the purposes of this report, we look at only the interest payment.

B) Speak to your accountant about the difference between a repair expense and a capital improvement. A major upgrade on the property will typically be regarded as a capital improvement and is dealt with very differently, from a taxation standpoint than a repair or maintenance expense. For the P&L statement, we look only at the repairs and maintenance.

C) The P&L statement provides you with GROSS profits, before "EBITDA" (earnings before interest, taxes, depreciation, and amortization). This is a measure of a company's profitability before your accountants do their thing to help reduce the taxes you pay.

RENT ROLL AND CASH FLOW ANALYSIS

With one property, calculating your combined rental income is pretty easy. It becomes more challenging as your portfolio grows.

A proper "rent roll" has the following items locked into one easy-to-read spreadsheet.

- Building address
- Unit number
- Tenant(s) name
- Date of occupancy
- Initial rent at date of occupancy
- Date of last rent increase
- Current rent
- Date of the next rent increase notice

It's pretty simple stuff. But with everything on one spreadsheet, it's super easy to keep a handle on your revenues. Forgetting to increase the rent on a certain date is equivalent to losing out on your business' revenues. You are the CEO of your business. It is very difficult to maintain or enhance bottom line numbers unless the top line numbers also continue to increase. No tenant will ever call you up to tell you that they haven't received their rent increase this year. It is your responsibility to do it (or assign it to someone else).

Insider Tip: We used to raise each tenant's rent on exactly the one-year anniversary of when they moved in. Over time, and as we grew our portfolio, that became a real pain. Now, we notify the tenants in the fall, give proper notice for our region, and then have the tenant's rent rise on January first or sometimes February first. By having all of the rent increases around the same time, it is easier to track and execute it, plus being in a cold weather part of the world, there is far less chance a tenant will vacate their unit because of the rent increase. By the time spring rolls around, they are likely more accustomed to the higher rent.

Landlords are usually pleased when tenants move out, as they can often rent it out for a higher amount, in States and Provinces with some level of rent control. However, I don't know one landlord that is excited when the tenant moves out in the winter and you need to scramble about to find a tenant on the coldest days of the year.

A **"cash flow analysis"** is a summary of all the money going into the business from the property LESS the amount of money going out of the business (mortgage payments and other monthly expenses).

As I have said previously, even if you are heavily leveraged, as long as the property is delivering positive cash-flow results, it won't matter that there was a market correction and the value of the property dropped, or you lost your job and don't have any primary income any longer; the property and the business will be self-sufficient. The business may have needed your income in order to qualify for the leveraged mortgage, but because the property has a positive cash flow, there is no need to supplement or prop up the business to keep it afloat. In fact, over time, as the revenue and cash flow improve, the business will even be able to support you.

TENANT SELECTION

We have dedicated an entire chapter to the subject of tenant selection, in Keep Your Sanity...Pick the Right Tenants. Obviously, this is a key part of your "part-time job" in running this business, but if you complete your due-diligence for each tenant applicant, there is no reason to believe that this will be a huge portion of your ongoing jobs.

The tasks in this chapter are necessary. Yes, real estate investing can generate relatively passive income for you and your family, but certain things are required to keep the revenue stream coming in. If you are unwilling or unable to take on these tasks, there are professional property managers, bookkeepers, handymen, and administrative assistants that can complete them for you. Yes, it might reduce or even eliminate the cash flow from the property, but it allows you to maintain the wealth-building instruments in your portfolio. By delegating some or even all these jobs, you still take advantage of the wealth built from the mortgage paydown, and any potential long-term appreciation.

But even with a full set of professionals at your disposal, you are the CEO of your business and ultimately you are responsible for the performance and safety of your investments.

The reality is that most weeks, depending on the size of your portfolio, you really shouldn't need to dedicate more than a couple of hours a week. It all starts with buying QUALITY PROPERTIES in QUALITY NEIGHBORHOODS, which attract QUALITY TENANTS. If you did that right, the ongoing work should be minimal.

Occasionally, I receive pushback from wannabe investors or acquaintances who tell me that they simply don't have the time to look for investment opportunities, or managing a portfolio. I politely reply that I suppose that building wealth isn't a very big priority in their life and if that ever changes, and they are looking to build wealth, then they can reach out to us.

Most of us in our early to mid-20s start working 40 hours a week, 2,000 hours a year. We join the "rat race" and deal with life's ups and downs HOPING that we can build up enough savings to retire in 40-plus years with enough funds that we don't go broke in our senior years.

This "part-time job" may mean that, along with your current full-time job, you are now working closer to 45–50 hours a week, but those extra few hours can allow you to leave the rat race 10–15 years earlier. Imagine being sure of your retirement plans, confident that you have the funds to live the life you want without depending on your 40-hour a week income, and being able to do that at age 55 instead of 65. As great as the extra wealth is, what real estate investing really offers you is freedom and choice. It gives you TIME.

Real estate investing is the part-time job that, when done properly, WILL make you a millionaire.

> *"Time is more valuable than money.*
> *You can get more money, but you cannot get more time."*
> *—Jim Rohn*

SUCCESS STORY
Sophie and Dylan Currie

Sophie and Dylan were both around 28 years old when they first considered investing in real estate. Both had been working for several years and were earning a solid and stable income. They already owned their personal residence, which they bought together while they were still dating. They were aggressive in mortgage paydown and it had appreciated some in that time.

They went to their friend and mortgage broker. Sophie had always believed in the expression, "You need money to make money." For the first time in their lives the equity in their family home had given them some money. Because of their mortgage situation, it made sense to hold off until the end of 2015 (nearly a year after first considering real estate investing) before they could access the funds through a refinance, so they used that time to learn more.

They attended local meet-ups and considered different investment strategies such as downtown condos. But after meeting with me at my favorite restaurant and second office, Los Cabos, and talking about wealth building using suburban two-unit dwellings, they were determined to move forward with that investment strategy. Investing in real estate made a lot of sense to them, as nearly all the wealth they had at that time came from the home they had bought about four years earlier. No other investment they had generated close to the same kind of return.

During their education process, they met with other investors, attended the Doors to Wealth investor tours, and continued to attend local real estate investing meet-ups. Finally, they were ready to take action. Because their finances were a tad limited, they chose to invest in an older home, one that needed some upgrades but already had a legal secondary suite. They realized that such a property would require more long-term TLC, but because of their lack of available funds, this was about all they could afford at the time.

Their families had never been wealthy, and none of their friends or family had ever invested in real estate. When they presented their plan to buy an investment property, it was met with immediate skepticism. Although they did nothing to sabotage the process, their friends and families certainly weren't supporters. They expressed concern about the risks, the level of work involved, dealing with tenants, and getting in over their heads.

But Sophie and Dylan did their research and understood real estate investing could be a means of wealth building for themselves and their eventual family. In fact, despite other people's negative reactions, because of the level of research they had done, when they eventually made the decision to buy that first property they considered it a "no-brainer, and there was very little stress involved."

Over the years, like all investors at some point, there were a few times when they briefly wondered what they were getting into and whether they were cut out for it. When a renovation they were working on went poorly, or in dealing with their one problem tenant, there were moments when they briefly pondered getting rid of the property. But they never seriously reached that point. They would always sit back and remember that they were doing it for their retirement and it was worth a little bit of work every once in a while.

About a year later they had amassed enough funds to buy a second investment property for their portfolio. They estimate that they spend a few hours a month on administrative tasks and bookkeeping, and occasionally a couple more hours a month on average for any minor maintenance. For the most part, though, the investments are running themselves.

Sophie stresses that owning the properties has had a significant impact on their net wealth. She admits that she really didn't even know what the term "net wealth" meant other than when she Googled famous people and saw how much they were worth. But after having met the Doors to Wealth Group, she now looks at their net worth portfolio every six months or so to see how they are doing and how their wealth is growing. Today, they also invest in equities and other investments, but the real estate holdings have been the driving force to building their net wealth to where it is today. Sophie shared, "It's staggering over the last five years the exponential growth that we're seeing because of the mortgage paydown—and that compounds over the years. It would be very slow gains if it wasn't for our rental properties."

A couple of years ago, Sophie and Dylan had a child. As most new parents do, they immediately started thinking about means of saving money for their son's college education. The amount was overwhelming. But it was reassuring to know that if it came down to it, they could sell or refinance one of their investment properties and basically pay for their child's education in full. "It's added a huge level of comfort and reassurance knowing that we have that piggy bank and we can tap into it for whatever reason. It's the best insurance policy you could ask for."

Right now, because they both have solid incomes, all their extra cash flow goes back into their properties and even mortgage paydown. At their age, they are more focused on building their wealth versus having the extra cash for a vacation or other expenditure.

Some of their friends have done side hustles like making scrunchies and doing odd jobs here and there. They tell their friends to forget about all that and go out and buy an investment property!

Finishing up, Sophie made sure to point out that investing in real estate and working with the Doors to Wealth team has changed the trajectory of their lives financially. "The openness and willingness to educate us with potentially no return or reward is something that we feel indebted to forever." She continues, "It's like the Rich Dad, Poor Dad book that everybody knows; our parents were never able to give us the tools and education we needed to really grow our wealth, so we are very grateful to the Doors to Wealth Team that actually gave us the insight we needed."

ARMCHAIR MINDSET PLAYBOOK

🌂 Passive income is "Income resulting from cash flow received on a regular basis, requiring minimal to no effort by the recipient to maintain it".

🌂 Owning a property has assets like a business, liabilities like a business, and clients like a business, therefore it is a business.

🌂 The six month inspection visits to your assets are an essential part of running your business.

🌂 Reducing or eliminating the amount of common area space for residents to share is a great way to minimize tenant interaction and thus potential tenant disputes.

🌂 Having separate bank accounts for each property is a great way to organize your revenue and expenses of each asset.

🌂 Having a year end income statement lets you, as business owner, know how much you earned or lost in the current or previous years.

CHAPTER 12

THE MILLENNIAL PROFIT

"Ninety percent of all millionaires become so through owning real estate. More money has been made in real estate than in all industrial investments combined. The wise young man or wage earner of today invests his money in real estate."
—Andrew Carnegie

I was asked a question recently. It was this: If I could pass a note back to my 20-year-old self, what would it say? It was 1985! I was just getting going after my Bachelor of Commerce degree. Movies from that year that I watched in the theatre included Rocky 4, The Goonies, The Breakfast Club, and one of my favorite movies of all time, Back to the Future.

If I had received that sports almanac of future events (you gotta watch the movie to understand that reference) and navigated through my life avoiding the pitfalls, I wonder if I would have become the person I am today. Maybe it's only because of some of those early experiences and mistakes that I have been able to grow and build real wealth.

If you're in your 20s or early 30s and reading this chapter, you are light years ahead of where I was back then. I would tell you this race to building wealth is a marathon, not a sprint. The "secrets" to building wealth haven't really changed in my lifetime. In fact, reading quotes from guys like Andrew Carnegie in the late 1800s tells me the same rules apply today that existed over a century ago. It gives me a little comfort that this is not some new fad idea. For over 100 years, purchasing QUALITY PROPERTIES has been a recipe for success. Let others trade in crypto currency, drive for Uber Eats, and make scrunchies on the side.

Starting on the path may include learning, saving, and networking. If it takes you another year or two to be ready to build wealth, then that is how long it takes.

Spoiler alert! This book, about secondary suites, is going to tell you that the "secret" I would have shared with my 20-year-old self is to invest in real estate. Specifically, we are talking about legal two-unit dwellings. Yeah, I know there are a lot of ways to build wealth in this world. But since I can't throw a 90 mph fastball, I have never invented anything, nor do I have any tech knowledge, real estate investing is about as good as it gets.

OK. Let's say you've been working full time for a few years now, and have saved a bit of money. You're sitting on about $50,000 in an assortment of cash, RRSP, and TFSA assets (Canada) or a 401(k) plan (US). You have a steady income and your credit score is starting to look decent. Congratulations on that. Too many North Americans are more focused on what car they want to drive, rather than how they can build some real wealth. It always amazes me that people will own a Land Rover and still have a Land Lord.

Below are some commonly asked questions.

How can I take my $50,000 and turn it into owning real estate?

You can probably qualify for a single-family townhome or condo. But if you move into it, although it will eliminate your rental expense, it won't allow you to have a tenant, generate income, and amplify your wealth. Don't get me wrong; buying that home puts you ahead of most of your friends, and if the residence is in a good location, over time, that asset will build you some wealth.

My recommendation for any first-time buyer entering the world of real estate is to consider making that first purchase a legal duplex or property with a secondary suite. You can live in the crappier unit (likely still better than your apartment or your parents' basement) but then rent out the other unit. This will reduce the cost of the mortgage and get you further ahead much quicker. The popular term for this strategy today is "house hacking." The strategy has been around forever; it has just rebranded under a catchier name.

But my mortgage broker said I can only qualify for a certain amount, and the two-unit dwellings are out of my price range. Is that true?

Maybe not. The cool thing about having a legal second unit is that you can use that potential rental income on your mortgage application to help you qualify for the property. If the "better" unit generates, say, $1,500 a month, depending on the lender, they may use anywhere from 50 percent to 100 percent of that rental income and add it to the monthly salary you already have. Shop around with lenders and try to get closer to the 100 percent mark. That combined number may qualify you for a bigger property.

Another upside in moving into one of the units is that, because the home will be owner-occupied, assuming you can qualify, the lender may require as little as 5 percent of the purchase price (keep in mind the mortgage rules are always changing). So your $50,000 would be enough to buy a $500,000 two-unit dwelling, with 5 percent down ($25,000) plus closing costs, with a bit of room to spare.

Let's do the math:

Purchase price $500,000

Down payment $25,000 (5 percent of the purchase price)

Mortgage $475,000 (plus any government-sponsored insurance)

Is this place your dream home? Probably not. But it is an asset that can really set you up for the future. Let's again say that the home had a value of $500,000 at the time of purchase. Because you received a high-ratio mortgage, the longest amortization you can receive is 25 years (in Canada). Over time, you keep adding cash, and perhaps eventually you move into the home you want to live in, but if you keep the duplex, and now rent out both units, that rental income will cover all of your monthly expenses, albeit with not much to spare.

WILL I HAVE TO DEAL WITH ISSUES WITH THE PLACE?

Sure, from time to time but it will be worth it. You keep it for 25 YEARS. Guess what happens after that time. If you never attempt to refinance the property, the mortgage is now paid off and the property has had 25 years of potential appreciation. Even if the place is growing at just 3 percent annually for 25 years, the property has now more than doubled. Your initial $500,000 has bought you an asset that is now worth more than $1 million. One property, which was a very occasional part-time job made you a MILLION DOLLARS.

That's the power of leveraging your wealth through real estate. You can complain it isn't fair that homeowners are offered such advantages that renters just aren't offered, but I can tell you it simply isn't going to change. In fact, across North America, governments are looking for MORE ways to encourage the next generation to get into homeownership, not fewer. Lenders in Canada are backed by government-sponsored programs such as CMHC and Genworth, in which borrowers essentially pay an insurance premium allowing the lenders to provide up to 95 percent of the value of a home for someone to move into. The US also offers programs designed to help people move into homes such as Freddie Mac, Fannie Mae, and Federal Home Loan Banks. If done well, these programs can really boost the economy. If done poorly, and people who should not qualify for homes are allowed to move forward, and they eventually fail, it can have significant repercussions on the economy, like what happened in the US, and around the world, in 2008.

According to the US Census Bureau, the home-ownership rate (which is the percentage of homes owned by their occupants) sat at 64.2% in 2018. Before you believe the hype that home prices are creating an entire generation of renters, let me share with you some perspective.

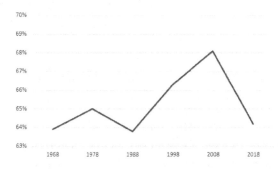

Chart 5: US Home Ownership Rate

Over a 50-year period, there has been a swing of about 4 percent of Americans in homeownership. In fact, the trend over the past 50 years is closer to 65 percent, which is about where we are now.

That said, it is fair to point out that the percentage of homeowners at age 30 is way down from previous generations. According to the Stanford Center on Longevity, in a 2016 study of homeownership, they compared the percentage of boomers to the percentage of millennials who owned their own home by age 30. The study found that for boomers, 48 percent owned their own home, versus just 36 percent of millennials.

There are a lot of reasons why the 30-year-old today is far less likely to own their own home. It may be due primarily to economic factors as, yes, home prices as a percentage of average annual salary are way up. But it may also be cultural, as homeownership seems to be less critical to the 30-something today than it was in prior generations.

But this book is about wealth building and despite two-thirds of your colleagues currently settling on renting or living with Mom and Dad, by approaching things a little differently, you have been able to save some money already. It has got you thinking that there must be a better way to build wealth. And finally, it has got you to pick up and hopefully purchase this book!

I don't want to end the discussion on leveraging without once more stressing that no lender, regardless of any insurance program, would even consider offering 80 percent financing (or more) of the purchase price of any investment with such a low interest rate unless they were absolutely convinced that it was a good business decision for them to proceed. Simply put, offering out loans to qualified recipients is a good bet by the lender. When done properly, the lender is confident they will get both their return on investment and even more importantly, their return OF investment.

Plus, according to the 2016 Census, 39 percent of Canadians own their home mortgage free. That means the ratio of mortgages in arrears to total residential homes in Canada is much lower. Don't let media reports trick you into thinking there is a lending crisis going on in our country. Sure, things could always improve, but there are simply no signs of Canadians losing their homes because they can't afford the mortgage payments.

Simply put, mortgage defaults are at historically low levels right now.

This is why lenders fall over themselves handing out low-interest mortgages, as they are confident they will be paid back. But even if they are not paid back the assets they are loaning against have real value and are a reasonable Plan B for the lender.

What does all this mean for me?

Real estate was a secure investment 100 years ago, 50 years ago, 25 years ago, and still is today. Federal, along with state and provincial governments want to keep homeownership levels strong. Policies are siding more and more with helping the next generation to buy a home. Take the programs offered and use the most leveraging you can afford to enter into the wonderful world of homeownership.

But the advantages don't end there. For pretty much any other investment, including investment real estate, if you can sell it for more than you bought it for, you must pay capital gains taxes on that investment. In Canada, capital gains are typically taxed at half of your earned income. So at your current salary, for every ADDITIONAL dollar of income you earn, you are subject to taxes of 40 percent, but if you sold an investment subject to capital gains, that would essentially mean those dollars are taxed at only 20 percent. In other words, if your investment made you $100,000, you would face a tax bill of $20,000.

Let me explain.

Base salary: $80,000 (what you make each year from working about 2,000 hours)

Amount you would pay in taxes on any amount over that: 40 percent (depends on where you live)

Profits from selling an investment: $100,000

Capital gains tax due on that investment: $20,000 (earned income would be $40,000, but capital gains is at least half that amount)

Capital gains tax due from selling an owner-occupied home with $100,000 of profit: that would be $0

This is an extremely rough illustration of the difference between investments with and without capital gains. As I mentioned earlier, the more you earn in that calendar year, the higher percentage you would pay THAT YEAR. Also, the overall tax rate varies greatly depending on where you live.

The US does things a little differently, allowing you to deduct the interest paid on any loan against your personal residence. That advantage too makes homeownership such an unfair advantage.

But is now a good time to buy real estate? With the [insert current issue or crisis] happening around the world and close to home, does it make sense to invest in real estate right now? Pick a year, any year. There will have been some sort of turmoil in that year. Something around the world that made the headlines. I am confident that there were some people out there who thought, "Now is not the time to buy real estate." Will there be bad shit that happens this year or next? Yep. Will there be strife around the world in 10 years' time? You betcha.

In this age of instant access to information from all over the world, it's easy to get sucked into the news stories of the day. Try to avoid the noise and focus on the trends that simply aren't changing.

Type in the words "rental crisis" and include an area that you think you would like to invest in. Keep in mind that nearly every rental article ever written is slanted on the side of the tenant's perspective. (Likely because the author of the article is a tenant him or herself.)

Ripped from the headlines: Vacancies Are at Generational Lows! Unable to Find Affordable Housing! Rental Increases Across the Country! Landlords Using the Technique of Renovictions to Increase Rent! These are real concerns across North America. Maybe you're currently experiencing these issues firsthand.

But instead of raising up your arms in frustration and accepting the situation for what it is, let's flip around the narrative.

We're talking about buying something, and eventually offering out an item that's in high demand. We can provide a product or service that the community desperately needs.

I will never recommend becoming some slum lord with below-standard rentals in need of repairs a term called "deferred maintenance," which means that the property owner knows they should fix something but puts it off for another time. There are a lot of rentals out there, where the property owner is more interested in short-term profits and offers a substandard property for rent. Short term, this can make some sense. Repairs can be quite costly. But long term, it affects the quality of tenants you can attract, which will lead to more abuse of your rental unit, which makes the product even worse, which affects the amount of rent you can charge, which limits the amount of profits you can make. You get the picture. This cycle continues until you either do the repairs or you sell the property. (By the way, a property in need of repair will sell for far less, so the deferred maintenance will also cost you in the resale.)

What I am talking about is becoming a rental housing provider of QUALITY HOMES in QUALITY NEIGHBORHOODS. When we look at housing and rental prices, we're not looking at a one- or even 10-year trend. We're looking at generation after generation of North American housing in good areas with proper market fundamentals.

Even if the cash flow is not quite what you were hoping for in the first year, if the property is in a desirable neighborhood, you can feel confident that you will not have much trouble finding a tenant, and that rental amounts will rise over time.

I try to teach my clients to make it a goal to get to three investment properties. If you can land three two-unit dwellings and live in one of the units, you have set your retirement wealth in motion. With a three-property portfolio, and 3–4 percent appreciation, it should take you about a decade to make that first million dollars in real estate.

Because you are limited in your available funds, it might make sense to target a first property in need of some repair. The plan is to force some appreciation in the dwelling, thus allowing you to be able to refinance it, and take out some available cash. Hopefully, it will be enough to buy property number two. Repeat the process one more time.

It might take you a few years and a heck of a lot of evenings and weekends working on the unit, because being so limited in funds, you are the one doing many of the repairs and updates yourself. While your friends are out partying and likely mocking you, it's YOU who chooses to stay in the home, fixing up the investment, and building some real wealth.

A Multi Generational household could be the way to go

OK. I'm sold on real estate, but there is absolutely no way I can swing the down payment for a number of years. What options do I still have?

The bank of Mom and Dad has been around forever. So many parents have helped out and got their children into real estate. The cool thing about real estate is this is not like that $200 you borrowed in your last year of college that you never paid back nor had any intention of ever paying back! This can be a joint venture type of arrangement. Parents can either have an ownership stake in the property or can offer an interest-bearing loan where the proceeds come from the revenue generated by the rented unit(s).

A joint venture can be a win/win situation. Perhaps your parents are doing "OK" but don't have too much in the way of retirement investments. With your newfound education, you can leverage their home equity into a situation where they now have some retirement assets, or monthly income.

Let me throw another scenario past you. Perhaps your parents are in a position to downsize from the family home. Maybe there are some health issues to deal with. Two-unit houses could allow you live with Mom and Dad without actually "living with Mom and Dad." Each of you can have your own separate dwelling unit. It's just that both of the dwelling units share a roof. Or there may be times when the parents want to downsize and travel and this allows them to have "an apartment" that they can leave whenever they like while the kids are there to maintain the house.

For whatever reason, multi-generational housing was popular long ago, but kind of fell out of fashion over time. In some cultures, it's far more common. In my case, I moved over four hours away from my folks just to avoid such a scenario. The thought of caring for my in-laws in their later years scares me more than you can imagine. But this is not about my situation! Besides, in today's housing market, we are seeing a growing trend in some circles to return to multi-generational living.

It may sound cliché, but when it comes to moving forward, you are only limited by your own imagination. Having said that, don't expect a risk-averse parent to agree to refinance their principal home that they have spent a generation paying off based solely on their kid's "whim of the day." Remember, these are the same people that were there when you told them you were planning on quitting school to start a band. They saw when you crashed the car into a ditch. They're still paying for your decade of dance lessons or rep hockey league fees.

If you really want to convince them that this is the proper strategy to set them up for their future, attend meet-ups, do your research, and include them in this journey to wealth building.

Don't be discouraged if they aren't immediately ready to take this journey with you.

Taking action comes in many forms. The obvious one is purchasing a property. But it may also include reading an investment book, attending a real estate meet-up, meeting other investors or perhaps people that will make up your future power team, adding cash for a future down payment, and so much more.

Wealth offers you freedom and choices. Although I don't know many people who wake up and say, "YES! I get to be a landlord," the freedom and choices offered can really make it all worthwhile. Simply put, owning investment real estate is a part time job that WILL make you a millionaire.

"If you live like no one else, one day you
will be able to live like no one else."
—Dave Ramsey

BONUS QUOTE!

"Put that cookie down, NOW!"
—Arnold Schwarzenegger,
from the movie *Jingle All the Way.*

Note: Admittedly, this quote offers no insight into the world of real estate investing, however, this has been and remains my son and my favorite Christmas movie. You may think that this is an odd choice to be a favorite, however, in the end of the movie, when the boy says he doesn't need the Turbo Man doll because he has the real Turbo Man at home, I cry every time.

I promised Jonathon I would try to work in the quote somewhere in the book. Here's hoping we all have a little Turbo Man in all of us.

SUCCESS STORY
Jason Shackleton

Jason was always a bit of a saver. Recently out of school, Jason worked full time at General Motors on the line. By the age of just 24, he had amassed about $30,000 in savings, which eventually allowed him to qualify for a mortgage.

Jason's goal for years had been to one day use the funds he saved to buy real estate. So he used nearly every dollar in his savings account, plus some from his Canadian registered retirement savings plan (RRSP) and merged them to form the amount needed for a down payment on a property.

Jason did some initial research to help determine what he wanted to eventually buy. He read books on house flipping, Robert Kiyosaki's *Rich Dad, Poor Dad*, and Don R. Campbell's *The Little Book of Real Estate Investing in Canada*. He then Googled local real estate investing information, and found some articles written by me. Jason reached out and we met for lunch where he laid out his plan for buying his first property.

Although the $30,000 is an awesome amount to have saved considering his age, in his market of choice it had some limitations regarding down payment. Jason understood that he probably couldn't afford a legal turnkey two-unit dwelling, so he focused his attention on more inexpensive properties, in other words, a single-family home, which offered the option of adding a basement apartment. The property he eventually chose wasn't in the ideal location; the house and the property needed a lot of work, and in order to meet Canadian lending rules, Jason needed to make this property his primary residence.

The process for getting that first mortgage was anything but smooth. Because Jason was determined to not seek out a cosigner from his parents, he ended up needing to go to three mortgage brokers. The first two told him he couldn't qualify on his own, but a third found a way to get him the funds. Jason understood that he could only qualify with a "B" lender at higher interest rates rather than the traditional big bank lenders. But still, he looked at it as an opportunity to take action. This allowed him to put in all of his available funds and buy his first property.

His parents had bought and renovated a cottage and built up some sizable equity as a result of that purchase but none of his friends, nor any of his family members, had ever bought an investment property before. But despite having no "road map" to follow moving forward, Jason was determined to figure it out.

Because he had a tight budget after the purchase, Jason knew that he would need to do a lot of the renovations himself. "Every single day after work, I would chip away at a really small task. Breaking down the renovation, one room, one job at a time. Slowly but surely, renovating the property. It took me way longer than most people take." Many of his friends and coworkers thought it was a little weird that every evening and weekend was tied up working on the property. Jason fully admits that he can get obsessed with things like this but he felt that "there was no real Plan B."

Jason needed to watch every dollar. Other than electrical and inspections, he didn't hire out any work to contractors. He did utilize his parents for free labor, but all the funds were his own. His mom became the "Kijiji queen," finding used building materials and other supplies they could use at little to no cost. They found kitchen cabinets for next to nothing provided they removed them from their current home. Appliances, flooring, and so much more they got at reduced amounts.

It took more than a year, but eventually Jason was able to meet the criteria set forth by the city and get his legal two-unit certificate. The sweat equity he had put into the project was converted to real cash when he was able to then refinance the renovated property to its current market value. In fact, he was able to pull enough cash out of the property to qualify for a second property. Essentially, Jason started the process all over again.

Another year, and a lot more blood, sweat, and tears later and Jason was able to convert his second property into a legal two-unit home. By the age of 28, he had three legal investment properties. He lived in one unit and rented out the other five units to tenants.

It was at that time that General Motors announced they were shutting down their plant and that Jason would be let go. Many of his friends and coworkers were panicked as they had no reserve funds; they would be desperately looking for work once the doors of GM finally shut. Jason was far less concerned.

Jason estimates his net worth has increased 15 times what it was before he purchased his first investment property. He has monthly cash flow coming in from his tenants. The skills he learned over the years while working on the properties took him in directions he never imagined four years earlier. He is now considering doing some contracting, maybe a joint venture with other investors, or something else pertaining to real estate.

Jason points out how glad he was that he took action when he did. Had he waited until he was a little older, he would have been let go by his employer and had no opportunity to qualify for a mortgage. Despite not knowing how to convert a secondary suite when he began, he committed to learn a little at a time. He asked questions when he didn't know the answers. Then he went out and did it.

His number one piece of advice to others just starting out is to self educate. It doesn't have to cost to get started. A few books, YouTube, and online research can get you all the information you need. Jason believes that if he hadn't taken action when he did, he doesn't know where he'd be now. It wasn't easy to qualify for the first property; he wasn't even sure if his Realtor or other professionals would take him seriously. But Jason didn't let these roadblocks stop him from reaching his goals. He encourages others to start the process, learn as much as you can about what you need to do, then buy something.

ARMCHAIR MINDSET PLAYBOOK

🌂 "House hacking" on your first real estate purchase is an excellent way to enter into the real estate market.

🌂 Overall, the percentage of homeownership is about the same as it has been over the past 50 years, however, the number of 30 year olds owning their own home has dropped significantly.

🌂 Home ownership offers an unfair advantage when it comes to tax advantages and government programs.

🌂 The "bank of Mom and Dad" has been around forever, but instead of borrowing the cash and never pay it back, offering them an investment opportunity can allow you to get started and offer them a safe return.

CHAPTER 13

THE MISSING MIDDLE

"You don't learn to walk by following rules.
You learn by doing and falling over."
—Richard Branson

O ne of the biggest challenges that most people face is simply over-thinking real estate investing. But as I've said in previous chapters, the formula is straightforward. Once you find somewhere that meets the criteria of a QUALITY market, the goal remains to find a QUALITY property within a QUALITY neighborhood in that market. It is then that you have a really good chance of attracting that QUALITY tenant. That tenant treats your property well and pays the rent. Generally, this makes it pretty easy on you as the property owner and encourages you to continue to hold on to the property for longer. It's this duration of keeping the asset that allows you to make a QUALITY profit.

But what if there are prohibitive municipal regulations in the market you choose? It has a strong and growing job base, rising population, rising house and rental prices, low vacancy rates, and is even close enough for you to easily manage it. The one thing it doesn't have is municipal bylaws allowing investors to create secondary suites. My first reaction is to suggest that you continue your search in a different market.

As the expression goes: You can't fight City Hall. While this is not entirely correct, it can be extremely difficult and certainly time-consuming.

This chapter goes against everything I stand for in the laid-back investing lifestyle, and I totally give you permission to skip this chapter as it may not ever pertain to your circumstances. However, there are many of you who feel the need to make a difference in your selected community to address that "Missing Middle" and believe that if you're not the one driving this change, then who else will?

OK. I warned you.

I don't consider myself an expert on "Missing Middle" housing in any way. It is because of this that I will be quoting articles written on the subject by experts across the continent. Think of this as the beginning of your study on middle housing and a source for links to some of the leaders in the field of densification in housing.

First, a little recap on housing needs and development opportunities.

The good news is that if your selected community does in fact have a rental shortage, rising rents, a growing population, and a real need for more units quickly, then there are probably other people in the community looking at options for improving the situation.

Even better news is that this issue is something that tenant advocacy groups, community leaders, and rental housing providers can all agree on. The simple truth is that a community needs more rental housing units if it is to grow. Ideally, some of those new units will be made available at affordable rental rates.

Unfortunately, new-build housing, whether it be a single-family home, duplex, or a large purpose-built multiunit residence is just so expensive to create. The rising cost of materials, land, and labor to build the units simply eliminates "affordable rental housing" as a legitimate option for investors. They would need to recoup their huge expenses and charge a rental rate high enough to cover those costs in order to make a profit.

If new-build construction can't provide rental housing relief, the

ONLY alternative is utilizing existing building stock. The great news is that the overall policy trend across North America is to densify existing housing stock to allow multiple dwelling units in what once was a single-family dwelling. However, changing zoning is a long, slow process.

If your community leaders have not allowed secondary suites and triplexes to be constructed in single family residential areas, it is because when these homes were built 40–100 years ago, they were zoned for single residential use only. The "old school" approach to development is a reluctance to change that use. It may be because of their own personal beliefs or in fear or respect of the current residents, who resist changes to their community. The ironic thing is that these same people often relish the additional services and activities that come from a larger community.

But the argument against densification remains: the homeowner bought the property in an area with an expectation of not having multiunit residential rental units on their street or in their immediate neighborhood.

The reason why the arguments against changes to the community don't hold any water, however, is as long as there is a growing population the community is always changing. Any growing community will see new schools, expanded roadways, increased services, and so much more.

My in-laws purchased a home in the 1950s. The house was on Harmony Road in Oshawa, Ontario. When they bought the property, it was at the edge of their city, actually situated on a dirt road. You could say that it was "rural." In the 1960s, the road was paved and made into a solid two-lane road. Over the next 20 years, this road would become an exit off the primary highway (Highway 401) leading to Toronto. Traffic lights were installed and it became a regional road from the south to the north part of the city. By 2000, the road had become an exit off another highway (Highway 407) and was eventually converted into a four-lane corridor through the city. In 50 years, my in-laws saw their quiet residential home turn into a house on one of the busiest streets in the city. As they got older, the variety store across the street became less and less accessible. The last time my father-in-law tried to cross the street, it was the equivalent of a real-life game of Frogger.

When they finally sold their home they had to factor in a discount to account for being situated on such a busy road.

Yet, despite this 50-plus years of dramatic developmental change, the zoning of their property remained residential. To be fair, the dramatic changes seen by my in-laws are unusual in most communities. But changes do happen. I am quite confident that in your designated market, there will be a similar street or series of streets that have seen modifications over the last 50-plus years if the population has been growing steadily.

SO, HOW DO YOU FIGHT CITY HALL?

It's rare that change happens in one big step. More likely, it will happen in a series of smaller, incremental stages.

Assuming you really do want to put on the hero cape and make a difference and I can't convince you to move on to another more accepting community, then let's discuss the strategy to get a community more densification-friendly.

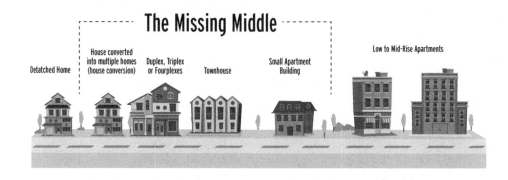

1. WHAT IS MIDDLE HOUSING DEVELOPMENT?

Middle housing is described as multiunit housing types such as duplexes to four-plexes, bungalow courts, or cottage clusters. These structures are typically not bigger than a large house and are often integrated into blocks with single-family homes. They are thought to provide more diverse housing choices and can help alleviate critical housing shortages and support community services such as public transit, schools, and more.

These buildings typically have a residential density of 16–30 units per acre, making them more dense than your typical standard residential community while still maintaining that community feeling that isn't possible with large multiunit buildings.

Pre-1950, this type of housing development was fairly common across many cities in North America. Then it just stopped. Municipalities began designing neighborhoods only allowing single-family homes. The dense communities were essentially just single-family, semidetached, and townhome options. The only alternatives to this was the permission to develop mid- and high-rise buildings, including both purpose-built rentals and condo buildings.

In 2010, architect and founder of Opticos Design, Daniel Parolek, first coined the term "the Missing Middle" referring to the lack of mid-sized densely built homes in communities across the continent.

He cited the primary reason for the lack of these homes was NOT the lack of demand but simply that communities en masse essentially made them illegal to build.

Debra Bassert of the National Association of Home Builders has said addressing missing middle housing can diversify and shift the direction of housing to meet the needs of varied income-levels and generations.[24]

From the site, www.missingmiddlehousing.com:

> *"Opticos Design is driving a radical paradigm shift, urging cities, elected officials, urban planners, architects, and builders to fundamentally rethink the way they design, locate, regulate, and develop homes. Americans want and need more diverse housing choices in walkable neighborhoods; homes that are attainable, sustainable, and beautifully designed."*[25]

We are fortunate to live in a country where we have a lot of freedoms. We can choose how we are to be entertained, we can choose the food we eat, we now have a choice of who we can marry, and what gender we choose to be identified as. During this time of such an incredible transformation of human rights, we remain restricted in our housing choices. Rules created in a different era, under different circumstances remain today limiting our choices of what home-builders can create, and homeowners can live in today.

2. WHEN YOU SAY "MIDDLE HOUSING," WHAT ARE WE REALLY TALKING ABOUT?

With few exceptions, these housing options share one property lot footprint and one property mailing address. They are not operating as condos and will have one individual property owner for the entire property.

The middle-housing objective is to enhance the number of options available to builders and homeowners when deciding what to do with their property. Here is a breakdown of densification options to consider. There are photos of each type of dwelling unit on our website www.armchairrealestatemillionaire.com, plus others that would be classified as middle housing.

Legal accessory apartment. This is a property built as a single-family home, but after occupancy, at some point a legal accessory dwelling unit was added to it.

Duplex. A PURPOSE-BUILT two-unit dwelling. Accessory apartments are often mistakenly referred to as duplexes, but because they were not purpose built, they are classified differently.

Triplex. A PURPOSE-BUILT property with three legal dwelling units in it.

Fourplex. A PURPOSE-BUILT property with four legal dwelling units in it. Can also be referred as a quadplex.

Legal nonconforming. In some municipalities and cities, occasionally properties are accepted with a certain number of dwelling units. Many of these properties have maintained their current use for more than 50 years. Zoning rules wouldn't actually allow the current usage, but because the property either pre-dates the zoning rules or exceptions were made regardless of the zoning status, it can then be named legal, even if it does not conform with the zoning bylaws.

Coach house. A dwelling unit situated typically above a garage or carport. Also referred to as carriage houses or garage apartments, they derived their name from the place where horse-drawn carriages were kept and the residence above that. Likely the most famous coach house came from the TV show Happy Days, where The Fonz happily resided for years.

Garden suite. A legal accessory dwelling unit typically located in the back yard of the principal dwelling unit. Thomas Magnum in the current reincarnation of Magnum P.I. lives in a garden suite. (Yeah, I probably watch too much TV.)

Laneway house. In some cities with typically narrow property lots, parking in the front or side of the house is simply not possible. Laneways are then created, running parallel to the main street, to provide access to the back yard, and so residents can park there. Often garages or car ports are situated at the edge of the property adjacent to the laneway. Some cities now allow homeowners to replace their garage, or rebuild it, adding a dwelling unit that fronts onto the laneway.

Tiny houses. This type of dwelling unit is extraordinarily popular right now, with TV shows featuring ways to maximize space. They are generally accepted to be under 400 square feet in space. They can be made from old trailers, converted garages, large sheds, or simply be purposely built. If zoning allows, a tiny house can be similar to a garden suite, with water and electrical access feeding off a primary dwelling. There is talk of creating tiny houses as a means of combating the homeless crisis in North America, with a piece of land allowing for multiple tiny homes, acting a little like a trailer park. [26]

Cottage clusters or bungalow court. A group of small, detached homes clustered around a central outdoor common space. Typically, some of the homes face the common area, while others face the street.

Other terms you should be aware of include:

Up-zoning. The term for allowing middle housing where currently only single-family housing is allowed. It can also apply to middle housing, or mid-rise apartment units that now qualify for high-rise developments. Essentially, everything in the community moves up a zone or two in terms of densification allowances.

NIMBY. An acronym for "Not in My Back Yard." It represents a segment of the population that doesn't want changes in their neighborhood.

YIMBY. An acronym for "Yes in My Back Yard." This is a recent movement by city residents and developers who are now pushing governments to allow them to build more and more housing.[27]

Lastly, I wanted to include alternative densification options that are increasingly being applied across North America. Some are newer ideas, while others have been around for generations.

Stacked townhouses. Townhouses are separate dwelling units that are linked together and share common walls. Stacked townhouses are set up so that one dwelling unit may have the lower level (basement level) and the ground floor while its neighboring unit uses the second and third floors, creating multiple single-family homes stacked one on top of each other. The ownership of this property may be within a condo corporation or may be freehold-owned with some common shared elements. This type of housing complex usually has individual mailing addresses.

Shared housing. Renting out a room, having a border, or adding a flatmate are living arrangements that have been around forever. Over the last decade, partly because of increases in rental prices in some markets and the surge of websites that specialize in short- and long-term rentals, shared housing has become much more popular. I don't need to spend time speaking about the merits of this style of densification and affordability, as they have been written about many times by people far more knowledgeable on the subject.

Co-ownership housing. Also known as shared ownership or joint tenancy. It means you buy a share of a house, pay a mortgage on that bit of the house, and live in the house with others who may have the same ownership stake in the property. This commune-living lifestyle was popularized by the 1960s "Flower Child" generation. Due to affordability concerns, co-ownership is having a bit of a resurgence of late.

Condo housing. A condominium is often shortened to a "condo." It's a type of living space similar to an apartment, but independently sellable. The condo building structure is divided into several units that are each separately owned and surrounded by common areas that are jointly owned. Condos are not limited to high-rise and mid-rise complexes but can also be found in townhouse complexes and other community housing complexes.

3. LEARN WHO THE PLAYERS ARE

In the sports world, teams study their opponents very closely. They know their strengths and weaknesses. Similarly, in the community relations world, you need to learn as much as you can about all your local councillors. Watch and attend council meetings—you will quickly see a trend in what they believe and support. Try to meet up with the councillors most likely to support your causes. Perhaps customize your eventual proposal to better be in line with councilmembers' causes.

Meanwhile, begin to learn the "players" who can act as tenant advocates. Which organizations would benefit from improving the safety and affordability of additional rental units? Again, meet with as many of these people as you can to get a better handle on what their goals are and try to structure your proposal to align with those goals.

4. THE POWER OF THE COMMITTEE

Politicians love forming committees. You now speak their language. The goal is to bring a lot of smart people together to find ways to make a real, lasting difference in the community by creating and improving the quantity and quality of legal affordable housing.

Include densification ideas in your proposal. Ideally, by co-authoring the proposal with other community leaders, your proposal has a better chance of moving forward. The process varies by community, but typically a committee will fall under developmental services or a city council meeting. If you're part of creating a committee you can also be part of the solution.

5. WHY DID MIDDLE HOUSING DISAPPEAR?

In housing communities built between 1900-1940, middle housing was extremely prevalent. The early 1940s was scarred by WWII, but post-war, there was a huge demand for housing as soldiers returned home. Cities, states, and provinces started to create freeways to expand housing development outside the city. In short, the suburbs were born. They developed zoning regulations that separated regions by housing type.

But diving deeper, the 1940s and 1950s was an era of unchecked segregation between races and classes in North America. Yes, Canada wasn't quite as blatant as the United States, but segregation between classes certainly did (and does) exist.

According to a 2017 Washington Post article by Elizabeth Winkler, it can be easy for people to assume Americans want to live close to people like them—whether they're similar in race, socioeconomic status, etc. But there are other forces at play. Economic and racial segregation, according to the article, work to keep poor and working-class people out of primarily white and wealthy communities. Ordinances requiring single-family homes can be a tool to keep that segregation alive.[28]

Call me an optimist but I believe that once local, provincial, and state politicians, along with local media, understand the genesis of the zoning laws, including how and why they were created and how they (inadvertently or intentionally) were restrictive to certain segments of the community, the door will swing open a little and the community will work together to become more inclusive with regard to all, or at least more, of their resident citizens.

6. JUST THE FACTS, MA'AM

It's possible that I am too engrossed in the subject matter, however, as you will see in the examples to follow, it really feels like there is a continent-wide shift towards densification and up-zoning in major cities to combat outrageous home prices, rental rates, and homelessness prevalent across the nation. Admittedly, it's a slow shift; when it comes to housing, change rarely happens in major chunks.

I'm aware that the moment I quote any examples of changes in zoning rules in this book, they will become instantly out of date. I appreciate, however, that it's vital for you to have as much up to date information about densification trends across the US and Canada as possible. I suggest you head to www.armchairrealestatemillionaire.com for all relevant links as well as a glossary of terms you might find helpful regarding modifications made by municipalities allowing for more densification.

Remember that single-family zoning is practically a religion in most North American cities. Homeowners and local politicians who grew up in that community want to protect their neighborhoods and idyllic streets. Anything that doesn't meet their "Mayberry"-type community is thought of as wrong.

Times have changed, and the old guard is far more selective with their choice of words, but the sad fact remains that there is a segment of the population that just don't want "those kinds of people" living in their neighborhood. The goal is to combat NIMBYism across the country. There is a large segment of the population that believes in the benefits of urban growth, and likes to see their city add new amenities, but don't want that growth to impact them directly.

On a more positive note, there are some states and provinces that have tried to buck the curve and introduce middle housing into their cities. What follows are case studies from across the continent to better illustrate what some regions are doing about densification and how they're getting a handle on their lack of affordable housing in their communities. I finish with a case study of one of the greatest cities in the world and the challenges it faces because of a lack of affordable housing.

OREGON

In July 2019, the state's House and Senate passed House Bill 2001 that requires cities in that state to allow duplexes in areas zoned for single-family residential homes. In the Portland metro area, the bill goes even further, requiring cities and counties to allow the building of quadplexes and "cottage clusters" of homes around a common yard.

Despite pushback from many fronts, the bipartisan bill will allow builders and land-owners the option to create alternative buildings in areas that were once restricted to single-family homes. Although the press claims that the bill essentially bans single-family zoning, that is by no means the intention.[29,30] It is simply giving people the option to develop land in alternative ways.

The title of the bill, "Related to housing; and declaring an emergency," recognizes that the policy will not have any impact on state revenue and received support from the state support organization Habitat for Humanity and other community-based organizations.

According to the State of Oregon website when addressing the policy change:

"House Bill 2001 aims to provide Oregonians with more housing choices, especially housing choices more people can afford. The law, passed by the 2019 Oregon Legislature, lets people build certain traditional housing types, like duplexes, in residential zones. These housing types already exist in most cities but were outlawed for decades in many neighborhoods. These limitations contribute to increased housing costs and fewer choices. House Bill 2001 will require updates to local laws that currently limit the types of housing people can build.

MORE DIVERSE, AFFORDABLE CHOICES

People need a variety of housing choices. Today, too many Oregonians are paying too much for the housing they have and are limited to renting or buying detached single-unit homes. Also, the composition of Oregon households is shifting; more than a quarter of households today are made up of a single person living alone.

At different times in our lives we have different needs. Think about where a young adult might want or be able to afford to live, or imagine the needs of a retired person. These laws may help older adults remain in their neighborhoods and be near grandchildren, friends, and caregivers."[31]

Oregon has set the template for others to follow. The state recognizes that the changes in its municipalities will be gradual, and that municipalities will still have control of determining land setbacks and design requirements. There will still be certain regulations on providing adequate infrastructure such as sewers, water, electrics, and roads.

Tina Kotek, speaker of the Oregon House and author of the bill is quoted as saying, "Wages are up, people are working, unemployment is way down; and people can't find a place to live."[32]

Oregon, along with many states and provinces has long intended to protect farmland and green spaces beyond the cities. But despite this, many cities have been reluctant to densify within its city walls. Kotek continues, "In Oregon, the joke goes, people hate sprawl and density. At some point, something has got to give."

Prior to this policy change, 77 percent of Portland[33] was zoned for detached single-family residential homes. Although that percentage by no means leads the nation, it was certainly a trend that limited that city's growth and saw tremendous push back by segments of the community. Russ Axelrod, mayor of West Linn, Oregon, reacted to the bill by stating it was "stupid."[34]

No one is expecting the streets to be bulldozed overnight, with single-family homes being replaced by mid-sized housing options. But over time, old housing stock may be replaced, infill will occur, and homeowners will create additions allowing for secondary or tertiary suites on their property.

Oregon's Bill 2001 may become a landmark policy for the trend to lightly densify other cities across the continent.

CALIFORNIA

This state may just be at the epicenter of the affordable housing crisis in the United States,[35] combining population growth with limitations on urban sprawl because of the Pacific Ocean, mountains, and protected green space. A thriving economy and awesome year-round weather make California "the place you outta be, so you can load up the truck and move to Beverly."

The problem is that rising housing and rental prices are making finding an affordable home nearly impossible in many cities. San José, for example, actually has 94 percent of its city zoned as detached residential. Los Angeles is sitting at around 75 percent. San Francisco is around 70 percent.[36]

In 2020, at the time of writing California was trying to pass Bill SB 50. Much like the policies passed in Oregon, the hope was to eliminate the mandatory single-family zoning restrictions. It's opponents, claimed it would change life as they know it, and some tenant advocacy groups felt it wouldn't do enough to combat homelessness and overcrowding.[37, 38, 39]

I think most people are missing the point. Think of this as one more tool in the toolbox to help the housing crisis. Think of this as a compromise to residents of a community not wanting large apartment buildings overshadowing their back yards.

The California bill SB 50 suggested that in neighborhoods within half a mile of rail stations, ferry stations, and other transit hubs, mid-rise apartment dwellings of four to five stories should be allowed. In areas further from public transit and jobs, it would permit dividing homes into duplexes, triplexes, and fourplexes.[40]

Senator Scott Weiner, author of the bill, states that altering the zoning rules, "will create more of every kind of housing because we need more subsidized housing for low-income people. But we need more market-rate housing to bring down prices for people in the middle class." [41]

Critics fear that if all the new housing is "hyper-luxury housing" it will do little to help lower house prices for the middle class.[42] However, if more moderately priced housing is built, prices could decrease somewhat as owners and renters vacate their older housing stock, providing more affordable housing options to those who earn less.

This policy was not a cure-all option, as it won't singlehandedly eliminate the housing crisis across the state but if passed it will help alleviate the crisis to a small degree. Unfortunately, it didn't pass into law, but likely a similar proposal will follow in this state.

According to www.actionnetwork.org, a California-based group trying to add housing units throughout the state, "California's housing deficit is now equal to that of every other state combined." They are pushing for the signing of bill SB 50 for their climate, their children's future, and their state's future.

According to a 2019 New York Times article[43], city maps look a lot different now than they did in 1960. Back then, LA was zoned for about 10 million people. By 1990, according to the Times, LA downzoned to support only 3.9 million people. And the city is filling up. As of June 2019, it was at about 93 percent capacity.

The lack of mid-priced housing is forcing people out of the city. Although LA and the state of California have not yet stopped growing, the percentage of growth is certainly slowing down. Not because of a decrease in desire to live in the communities, but simply an inability to obtain housing.

Eventually, laws will be passed in the state allowing builders the right to develop missing-middle housing, but as they will also require city approvals, again, don't expect the changes to happen overnight.

ONTARIO

Canada's most populated province is also home to the fastest-growing major city in North America.

In 2019, the city of Toronto grew by about 77,000 people, more than the fastest-growing three American cities (Phoenix, Fort Worth, and San Antonio) combined. That kind of population growth requires 25,000–30,000 new dwelling units PER YEAR just to keep up.[44] This does not even consider the housing shortage crisis that already exists in Ontario cities.

In 2011, Ontario passed Bill 140, the "Strong Communities Through Affordable Housing Act" through the Liberal government, allowing homeowners the right to add secondary suites in detached single-family homes across the province.[45] Each city needed to pass their own set of bylaw modifications to accommodate the bill, but with little to no enforcement, some municipalities modified the mandate or simply outright ignored it.

In 2019, and under a Conservative government, the province passed Bill 108, the "More Homes, More Choices Act."

According to a 2019 Toronto Star article, Housing Minister Steve

Clark called for more middle housing.[46] A 2019 bill called More Housing More Choice would have allowed homeowners and builders to create secondary units. That could take the form of laneway homes, garages, and coach homes. The bill also made it so new construction homes wouldn't incur fees for establishing secondary units.

As of March 2019, according to the Toronto Star, zoning laws had a major impact on what could and could not be done in a residential neighbourhood.

Despite a high demand for housing, property owners are limited in what they can change. Property owners might be able to tear down one small house on a big lot to build two bigger houses with small lots, but they wouldn't be able to demolish one house to instead build a duplex or some other multiunit housing. Under the current law, property owners aren't able to make changes that would alter the feel and characteristics of a neighbourhood. That makes it difficult to address the affordable housing shortage.

Changing zoning laws would make it easier for new developers and current property owners to build beyond single-family homes.[47]

More than just permitting a totally new development, the altering of the zoning rules will allow existing homeowners to retrofit their existing homes. The obvious change carried out by most homeowners to date has been to build a basement suite, but if the rules allow, it will be possible to add a third suite with a new floor top up, a laneway home, a suite above or in replacement of a garage, a carriage home, or even an addition to the side or behind the existing home.

NEW YORK CITY

First the good news: Just 15 percent of New York City is designated as single-family residential, and the vast majority of that housing is in Queens. None of Manhattan remains zoned as just single-family. This has allowed the city to grow unlike any other for generations.[48, 49]

But despite the continual push for more densification, New York has eventually reached a breaking point where housing has become too expensive for too many people.[50] Eventually, all cities will reach this breaking point. The objective for growing cities might simply be to extend and delay that breaking point for as long as possible.

According to census numbers, in 2016, New York City peaked in population at nearly 8.476 million people. Over the following two years, 77,000 left, leaving Gotham City with populations in 2018 not seen since 2013.[51] "These estimates, of course, took place before the coronavirus pandemic created a major health crisis in New York. Not only did tens of thousands die, but The New York Times estimated that 420,000—roughly 5 percent of the city's population—fled town."

So what, you cry. New York remains the largest city in the country by far. This is true. But the lower population also means the Big Apple could reduce congressional representation, decrease demand in housing, and lower housing prices (this is already happening in some parts of the city). Is the city of Broadway, Times Square, Wall Street, and the Statue of Liberty simply too big to fail? Maybe, but unless the city can reverse the trend that began in 2015, expect the housing market to endure a sustained slump.

A lack of affordable low-income and middle-class housing has led to people deciding on places other than NYC to call home. With the trend moving away from working in the office every day, the option exists to live elsewhere and be able to actually afford a home.

It's too early to determine if this is simply a short-term blip, or a sustained trend, but it is absolutely something any large city should be watching closely. Although there is only one city quite like New York, the lesson remains the same whether you're talking about San José, California; Portland, Oregon; Minneapolis, Minnesota; or Toronto, Ontario. The good news is that in these cities, filling the missing middle of housing is still a viable option to allow minor densification and more dwelling units into their communities without adding any more urban sprawl.

FINISHING UP

As you can see, changing the attitudes of generations of residents will not happen overnight. I reiterate that, in theory, it's a fight worth pursuing. I'd love to see more younger Canadians and Americans spend a little less time focused on the use of plastic straws and more time on macro issues such as national debt and affordable housing.

Although it's a far more complicated issue, it will have a real and lasting effect on their lives. My hope is that young renters will focus their anger and protests away from the property owner, who is only trying to afford the expenses on his or her building, and transfer their attention to government bureaucracy and the fundamental policies that created the housing shortfall in the first place.

I started the chapter advising you to move onto a more investor-friendly community if your initially selected market doesn't allow you to "duplex" your dwelling unit or allow you to cash flow on each of your properties.

I stand by this advice at the end of this chapter. I encourage you to "fight the good fight" and join or start the YIMBY movement in your community. However, recognize that it will likely take YEARS of effort to accomplish the goal of densifying your community, if EVER it happens.

Even if you choose to never battle with city leaders, hopefully this chapter gives you some background and perspective on North American housing. If you use social media sites such as Twitter, consider unfollowing the Kardashians or other influencers and spending more time following news reporters and newsmakers in subjects that can directly affect you. You are welcome to begin your research on our website www.armchairrealestatemillionaire.com and follow the links, read the stories, and grow as an investor.

This should not prevent you from building your portfolio empire in another market, even if it is a few towns or even a few states or provinces away. The experience you will gain and the wealth you will build will give you credibility when you finally do "take on City Hall."

"Here's to the crazy ones, the misfits, the round pegs in the square holes…the ones that see things differently. They are not fond of rules. You can quote them, disagree with them, glorify or vilify them, but the only thing you can't do is ignore them because they change things, they push

the human race forward, and while some may see them as the crazy ones,
we see genius, because the ones who are crazy enough to think they can
change the world, are the ones who do."
—*Steve Jobs*

ARMCHAIR MINDSET PLAYBOOK

🌂 There are others in your town or city that share your views on more affordable rental housing. Find those people.

🌂 Middle housing is described as multiunit housing types, from duplexes to four-plexes, bungalow courts or cottage clusters and are not much bigger that a large single family home.

🌂 Upzoning allows developers that were once restricted in areas to only develop single family homes, to now allow them to build middle housing developments.

🌂 The Oregon model is worth watching and over time we will see what effects it had on the communities and the housing/rental values.

🌂 There are at least six references to TV shows in this chapter.

CHAPTER 14

BUILDING YOUR DOORS TO WEALTH

"A Quality Property
In a Quality Neighborhood
Gets you Quality Tenants
Leading to Quality Profits"
—Michael Dominguez

The temptation will be there to purchase the cheapest property on the market. If you do end up finding a network of active real estate investors, the pressure will be on to "take action" and compete in a race to buy the most properties. Others will invest in inferior markets that are not likely to ever see population growth and stand little chance of increasing in value.

At the end of the day, the only race you are in is the one to improve quality of life for yourself and your family. Yes, you can build wealth by purchasing every "slumdog" building in some rundown town in the middle of nowhere. Yes, investors have been successful by using numerous joint-venture money partners and creating an entire enterprise where you are the CEO of a corporation or series of corporations that occupy your every waking moment.

But real estate investing doesn't have to be a full-time job. Don't get me wrong; if you want it to be a full-time career, that's great. But the purpose of this book, and this concept, is **to allow real estate investing to help fund your life, not run your life.**

Real estate investors don't need to look like the Monopoly man and wear the top hat, smoke the cigar, and drive the classic Mercedes Benz. Real estate investors are everyday people, from any age group, any social background, any demographic, any level of education, any previous economic background, from any hometown, and any upbringing. There simply is no template of what a real estate investor looks like and acts like.

In fact, in my experience, real estate investors are nowhere near the stereotype of some slumlords taking advantage of the innocent tenants who pay them money every month and get little in return. Investors are generous with their time, and their money. They share their knowledge and their experiences. It took me years to figure this out, but in life it doesn't have to be a "me versus you" mentality.

There is an unlimited amount of wealth in this world. I once thought that the wealthy were those 1 percent who wouldn't want someone like me to join their club. As I started to climb the ladder, I felt I would get kicked back down by the wealthy as they wanted it all for themselves. As I began to have some early success, however, I learned that the leaders ahead of me were instead reaching behind them and offering me their hand and their ideas and encouraging me to join them on the next rung of the ladder. I was skeptical at first that these successful individuals would use some of their valuable time to help me on my journey. However, over time, I learned that this really was the case.

I encourage all of you to find your networking group and your mentors. It's essential to build a team of like-minded individuals around you who are card-carrying members of TEAM YOU and are willing and able to work on helping you to build your success.

I intentionally chose success stories from people with varied backgrounds and who purchased a wide range of properties. While I have clients and friends with DOZENS of properties, who work full time managing their portfolio, their stories are not the point of this book. I specifically included investors with as little as two or three cash flow–generating properties to their name.

Sure the investors with 10 or more QUALITY properties are seeing some incredible success, but the investors who have even two properties are now in a strong position to raise a family, work in a full-time career, and know that the efforts they have made up to this point in their lives have put them in a comfortable position for their retirement, their recreation, and their family's future. None of them would be scrambling if they were let go from their job or the entire world's economy was shut down because of some kind of global pandemic (not that something like that would ever happen ...).

It's mind-blowing to me that a 30-year-old could buy ONE investment property for, let's say, a value of $400,000 to $500,000. Through leveraging, that person only needed to come up with a small percentage of that purchase price— even if they did NOTHING else in the real estate world, nor saved another dollar through equities or any other investment vehicle. As long as this person never refinanced that property and just kept renting it out, generating enough revenue to cover the monthly expenses and repairs, at the end of 30 years, that property would be completely paid for through the tenant's rent payments. If that individual was smart enough to have chosen a market to purchase the home in that appreciated at a rate of 3–4 percent annually (certainly not an outrageous appreciation rate in a growing community) then the property value would be at least double what they paid for it and possibly much more.

This individual, who scrounged every nickel they had to come up with a down payment on an investment property when they were 30 years old, then did absolutely no other investing or saving for the next 30 years, as they turn 60 years of age has an asset worth more than $1 million. (It might help to say that part in the voice of Dr. Evil from the Austin Powers movies).

Sure, you can make the claim that $1 million won't have the same level of importance in three decades' time, as inflation will raise the prices of everything. But we all know we can't count on government programs to support us. I would much rather have a plan in place that can practically assure me of being a millionaire than leave it up to chance.

The goal I gave you at the beginning of this book is to one day get up to three investment properties. If you want to grow beyond that, awesome. But with just three investment properties, you can set yourself up to fund your lifestyle, decide when you want to retire, have the freedom to do what you want to do, and create a legacy that can be passed onto the next generations of your family. Or you could give it all away to the charity of your choice.

The secret formula begins with that QUALITY PROPERTY in a QUALITY NEIGHBORHOOD, which you then combine with TIME. There are properties I bought below market value, and there are properties some might even say I overpaid for at the time. Sure it's important to get a fair price for the property, but if you bought that really good property and you were able to bring in outstanding tenants who took care of your units and paid their rent on time, and you were able to create a relationship of mutual respect, then holding on to that property for years and years won't seem like such a burden. To that 30-year-old investor in the example above, did it really matter at the end of the day if the property they bought was $450,000 or $470,000 when 30 years later the mortgage is paid off and the place is worth over a million dollars? True, $20,000 seemed like a big deal at the time, but imagine if it made the difference for that investor of choosing not to move forward on a great property. What a loss that would be.

I've been in this game long enough to see the discounted properties in mediocre neighborhoods that advertise stronger cash-flow potential come and go on the market. The interesting fact is that the worst of the properties often seem to come available every 2–4 years. If the property were really delivering the cash-flow profits promised at the time of purchase, the investor wouldn't be selling just a few years later. Too often, years of deferred maintenance, combined with sub-optimal tenants make this investment more trouble than it's worth. Instead of dealing with the issues and investing the money to bring the property up to current standards, it's easier to pass it off to the next guy and again offer the potential of great cash flow and returns to the next unsuspecting sucker.

The formula is simple. Maybe too simple for some. I get that. We have been taught our whole lives how difficult it is to build wealth and get ahead. Wealth management equity companies advertise their services and tell us to give them our money as they have really smart people who understand this stuff and have extensive algorithms that can do a much better job at managing your money. It's all crap.

No one is more dedicated to your success than you are. Just because one path to success includes swimming in a pool of crocodiles, then navigating through a jungle of poisonous snakes and killer bees, doesn't mean that this is the only path to success. Perhaps, just perhaps, there is a path that can avoid all of that. There may be a bed of roses along the way and yeah, there are some thorns to avoid, but it's a much simpler, safer, and more proven way along the path to success.

If you have made it this far in the book, I thank you and congratulate you. I hope that some of what I shared will resonate with you. I encourage you to continue with your financial education. Read more books on the subject, attend seminars with other like-minded individuals, listen to podcasts, watch YouTube videos, and begin to follow other investors on Twitter and Facebook.

Sure, it's fun to watch that cat video or follow that TikTok dance craze, but these are all distractions. Maybe just once, put down People magazine or shut off The Bachelor on TV and spend a little time on self-education.

Twitter and Facebook can be outstanding sources of education and knowledge. The key is to only follow like-minded investors, journalists, businesses, business leaders, real estate magazines, and similar sources. Don't hesitate to subscribe to newspapers and publications that you find valuable. If you find someone you follow is venting for the hundredth time about some political leader or some insignificant controversy that will distract you or even anger you, then get rid of that distraction.

I encourage you to follow myself and the Doors to Wealth Real Estate Group on Twitter and Facebook. If you like what you see, we invite you to register to receive our monthly Investor Report e-newsletter. It will have some local content that may or may not be relevant for your personal investment journey, but there is always a focus on positive strategies for moving forward. We congratulate success and try to motivate our readers to take action. Because we have been doing this for a long time, we have a fairly extensive list of like-minded investors and investor real estate agents in our database. Even if you have little to no interest in ever investing in the areas that our group services, we hope that you will connect with us anyway.

The real estate investment community may seem like a massive, scary group, but the more you get to know them, you begin to realize that it's a close-knit community, where people have shared interests and goals. We encourage you to reach out to us. We are more than happy to make the introductions to get you started in your communities of choice.

My mentors would slap me on the wrist when my ideas began to sway me from my ultimate goals. When my plans included ventures that put my entire portfolio at risk, I had someone to steer me away from those decisions and stay on the right path. My path was a little boring at times, which may have been one of the reasons why I was looking for the adventure. Make sure you too have someone who is willing to slap you on the wrist, either literally or metaphorically, and tell you that your idea is far too risky.

Hey, I'm that "C" student who struggled to get through school. I was never thought of as the go-to person to steal your homework from. The cool thing about real estate investing is that it doesn't matter what your grades were in high school; it doesn't matter that your boss won't give you that promotion because he doesn't think you are management material; and it doesn't matter that you have had failed relationships or a crappy childhood.

What matters is what you do going forward. It matters that you begin your journey in your financial education. It matters who you begin to network with and the content you put into your brain everyday.

As the classic quote states, "The journey of a thousand miles begins with a single step." Consider the reading of this book a great first step. Refocusing your social media content is another simple step to take. Searching for AND ATTENDING local meet-up investor groups where you have the chance to meet similar minded individuals, another good step.

I want to end with the reminder that although each step is vital, do not forget the adage of Michael Masterson's "Ready, Fire, Aim". You can analyze every property, every opportunity, speak to every other investor. There is ALWAYS, and I mean ALWAYS, a reason not to take action. From the new attendees of the meet-ups, to the people who are now completing their twentieth book on real estate investing, and to the people who just like the networking, there are no "participation medals" in wealth building. The winners are the ones who actually take action, follow their research, and buy something.

Thanks for 'taking action' and reading this book! Congratulations on that step, now go out and make things happen all while sitting in your comfy armchair!

ARMCHAIR MINDSET PLAYBOOK

☂   Real estate investors are everyday people, from any age group, any social background, any demographic, any level of education, any previous economic background, from any hometown, and any upbringing.

☂   Investors I know are generous with their time and their money.

☂   There is an unlimited amount of wealth in this world. it doesn't have to be me versus you.

☂   The secret formula begins with a QUALITY PROPTY in a QUALITY NEIGHBORHOOD, which you then combine with TIME.

☂   There is always, and I mean always, a reason not to take action. The winners are the ones who actually take action, do their research, and buy something.

ACKNOWLEDGEMENTS

I have a ton of people to thank for helping me get to where I am today and putting me in the position where I can share my knowledge with you, my reader. I don't know if I am ever going to write another book, so I apologize in advance, as I do have a lot of "shout-outs" to give.

I can only start with one person. I want to thank my wife, Lisa Coulter-Dominguez. It has been a little over 15 years since we first met. In that time, you have allowed me to grow as a person and in business. When we met I was stuck in a management position in a retail chain. I don't think I ever would have had the nerve to start my own business, invest in real estate, or invest in myself and grow towards my potential if I hadn't had you by my side to help.

Next up, I want to reach out to my son, Jonathon Dominguez. I spent a ton of hours and gave up a lot of evenings learning and building my business. I want to let you know that a big motivation for me was to get to a point where I can one day pass a part of my real estate portfolio to you. To be part of giving you a head start in life has always been a driving force.

I want to thank my "success story" participants for sharing some personal details with me and my readers. In no particular order: Karen Jackson, Jason Shackleton, Paul and Marlene Liberatore, Sophie and Dylan Currie, Winter Ng and Sophia Lee, and Anita Bongers-Lewis and Kris Lewis. I am really proud of you guys and am so happy for the success you have had thus far. I am pleased that I have been a small part of your success, and know that as time goes on, the success will keep compounding.

I have to give special recognition to Debbi Guislain. Lisa and I met her in 2006 when we were looking to buy our "forever" house. She recognized something in me and throughout the buying process, convinced me to consider getting my real estate license. I know I never would have even considered moving in that direction had it not been for her efforts. In addition, her mentorship in the early years helped lead me on my path.

Speaking of mentors, I've had far more than my fair share over the years. The list has to start with Don R. Campbell. I never had someone with his credibility and success take me aside and encourage me and teach me the way he did. He has played such an important role in my development as a Realtor, investor, educator, and as a person. Yes, he is the one who slapped me for straying off-course.

Another mentor along the way is Brian Buffini. His teaching and coaching program was top notch and the message was exactly what I needed to hear. Mike Montagano was one of the first Realtors I did a deal with. I remember him literally putting his arm over my shoulders and saying, "Michael, if there is one thing you need to do as a Realtor, it is to buy real estate." My Uncle Bill Stonkus was someone who would sit down with me in my early years and vent to me and teach me the way to be an entrepreneur.

Tahani Aberdeni recognized my potential even before I did. I remember her telling me early on that one day I would reach a certain level of real estate commission. I kind of laughed it off as that number seemed unattainable. Years later, when I passed by that number, I sent her an email letting her know I had reached her expectations of me. I knew David Mooney long before I ever considered investing in real estate. He taught me so many skills about equities, dividends, and investing that I use to this day. I met Russell Westcott through the REIN group and his passion and dedication to teach others have really rubbed off on me. I just hope that when I share my experiences, I can be even close to as captivating as Russell was to me.

There are business professionals, writers, and mentors that have shared so much. They may not know who I am, but I certainly have tried to learn as much as I can from their teaching. Leaders such as David Chilton, Warren Buffett, Robert Kiyosaki, Jim Rohn, and Kevin O'Leary. None of these great people may ever read this acknowledgement, but that doesn't change their importance in my development.

I need to thank the Re/Max Jazz team for all their kindness and support over the years. Special recognition goes out to my managers, Noel and Dave Coppins. Noel has been my go-to person for creative ideas. I have never met anyone with her level of passion and ability to be creative and come up with outside of the box ideas. Noel was a big part of the creation of the "Doors to Wealth Real Estate Group" brand. Dave has been a business leader and whenever I need to bounce a business idea off someone, Dave is the guy I choose. I should also thank Scott White and Lisa Nicole Smith. They have known me since the beginning, the "Dominguez: The Early Years" of my real estate career. Scary stuff.

Speaking about Doors to Wealth, I want to thank my team, past and present, for being such an important part of my life. My first hire in real estate was Cheryl Clai She has been integral to the team, even before there was a team. I thank you and respect you likely much more than you know. I also want to recognize Anita Bongers-Lewis and Jeff Whelan. I hope that I have given you as much as you have given me.

I want to reach out to my real estate joint-venture partners. Gino Siciliano has been my partner in crime in a bunch of deals. I am so glad to have you as a sounding board as we have both built our mini real estate empires. My other business partners, Tony and Kim Myers, Dave Steinbok, and Justin Cole, have all been part of one real estate deal, but their friendship goes well beyond that transaction.

A special shout out goes to the people at Durham REI and the REIN group. The level of education, networking, and friendship can not be overstated. I wish for anyone reading this to find a group of people that can help you grow your business as well as grow as a person. Quentin D'Souza, from Durham REI, and Patrick Francey from REIN; your leadership in your groups say a lot about the people you are. The number of people that you two have helped along their path is likely far more than you will ever know. If someone ever needed a real estate coach, you would be the guys I would always recommend.

I'd like to thank the number of superstar clients of mine that have been on the Doors to Wealth investor tours, who have not only been good investors, but friends too, and who have become mentors for the younger generation of investors. I want to recognize leaders such as Tom Sullivan, John Kim, Allen and Anna Castaban, Sheila Coleman, Sarah Coupland, Victor Huang, Jason Maahs, Michelle Palma, Aylmer Ng, Derik Smits, Jim Spridgeon, Craig Porter, Jesus Tavarez and Susan Hoo, Paul Tibbenham, among others. I am sure I left off a few stars and for that I am sorry.

I also want to give a shout out to my great friend and original contractor David Crosby. When I was getting started, I could write a series of books on the things I didn't know. David came to my rescue more times than I can count. The urine and cat shit story in the book came from David's efforts.

The other "service professionals" that I have worked with as part of my power team that has allowed me to continue to grow include Bob Durno (Premier Home Inspectors), Shelly & Cassandra Patrick (Thinkflame web designs), Mary Johnson (Dominion Lending), George Dube (BDO Dunwoody) and Guy Polley (Mack Lawyers).

I want to finish up with the Book Launchers team. You encouraged me—and also properly nagged and kicked my butt when needed. You dealt with my concerns and insecurities like true professionals. I encourage anyone who is considering writing a non-fiction book to contact Julie Broad and the Book Launchers team.

"There is no such thing as a "self-made" man. We are made up of thousands of others. Everyone who has done a kind deed for us, or spoken one word of encouragement to us, has entered into the make-up of our character and of our thoughts, as well as our success."
—George Matthew Adams

ENDNOTES

1   "U.S. retail vacancy rates 2019-2020," Statistica, accessed June 16, 2020, https://www.statista.com/statistics/194102/us-retail-vacancy-rate-forecasts-from-2010/.

2   Vicki Howard. From Main Street to Mall: The Rise and Fall of the American Department Store (Philadelphia: University of Pennsylvania Press, 2015).

3   **Hayley Peterson.** "More than 7,500 stores are closing in 2020 as the retail apocalypse drags on. Here's the full list," Business Insider, August 17, 2020, https://www.businessinsider.com/stores-closing-in-2020-list-2020-1.

4   Abha Bhattarai. "Malls are dying. The thriving ones are spending millions to reinvent themselves," Washington Post, November 22, 2019, https://www.washingtonpost.com/business/2019/11/22/malls-are-dying-only-these-ones-have-figured-out-secrets-success-internet-age/.

5   Troy Adkins. "The Rise, Fall, and Complexities of the Defined Benefit Plan," Investopedia, updated November 11, 2019, https://www.investopedia.com/articles/retirement/10/demise-defined-benefit-plan.asp.

6   Frederick Vettese. "The extinction of the defined benefit pension plans is almost upon us," The Globe and Mail, October 4, 2018, https://www.theglobeandmail.com/investing/personal-finance/retirement/article-the-extinction-of-defined-benefit-pension-plans-is-almost-upon-us/.

7   "Canada's Federal Debt," DebtClock.ca, accessed June 16, 2020, https://www.debtclock.ca/.

8   USDebtClock.org, accessed June 16, 2020, https://www.usdebtclock.org/.

9   Cameron Huddleston. "Survey finds 42% of Americans will retire broke—here's why," CNBC, April 11, 2018, https://www.cnbc.com/2018/04/11/gobankingrates-survey-finds-42-percent-of-americans-will-retire-broke.html.

10 Jamie Mauracher and Melanie Zettler. "Toronto's affordability crisis: How residents are being forced out of the city they love," Global News, March 25, 2020, https://globalnews.ca/news/6575583/toronto-affordability-crisis/.

11 Jill Cowan and Robert Gabeloff. "As Rents Outrun Pay, California Families Live on Knife's Edge," The New York Times, November 21, 2019, https://www.nytimes.com/2019/11/21/us/california-housing-crisis-rent.html.

12 "Leverage," Investopedia, accessed June 16, 2020, https://www.investopedia.com/terms/l/leverage.asp .

13 Lyle Adriano. "Study: Water damage claims surging," Insurance Business, March 11, 2019, https://www.insurancebusinessmag.com/us/news/breaking-news/study-water-damage-claims-surging-161741.aspx.

14   "Water Damage By the Numbers," Water Damage Defense, accessed June 17, 2020, https://www.waterdamagedefense.com/pages/water-damage-by-the-numbers.

15   Daniel Henstra and Jason Thistlewaite. "Climate Change, Floods, and Municipal Risk Sharing in Canada," IMFG Papers on Municipal Finance and Governance, Munk School of Global Affairs, No. 3, 2017, https://munkschool.utoronto.ca/imfg/uploads/373/1917_imfg_no_30_online_final.pdf.

16   Anna Momigliano. "The Flooding of Venice: What Tourists Need to Know," The New York Times, updated December 23, 2019, https://www.nytimes.com/2019/11/20/travel/venice-flooding.html.

17   "Effects of Hurricane Katrina in New Orleans," Wikipedia, accessed June 17, 2020, https://en.wikipedia.org/wiki/Effects_of_Hurricane_Katrina_in_New_Orleans.

18   Princeton University. "100-year floods will happen every 1 to 30 years, according to new flood maps," Phys.org, August 23, 2019, https://phys.org/news/2019-08-year-years.html.

19   Katie Dangerfield. "'100-year floods' are increasing in Canada due to climate change, officials say—is this true?" Global News, April 26, 2019, https://globalnews.ca/news/5206116/100-year-floods-canada-increasing/.

20   CTVNews.ca staff. "Quebec homeowners say $200K offer to relocate from flood-prone areas isn't enough," CTV News, April 23, 2019, https://www.ctvnews.ca/canada/quebec-homeowners-say-200k-offer-to-relocate-from-flood-prone-areas-not-enough-1.4391692.

21   "Florida's Sea Level Is Rising," Sea Level Rise, accessed June 17, 2020, https://sealevelrise.org/states/florida/?gclid=CjwKCAjw_qb3BRAVEiwAvwq6VoXGM7C00ltv-szzH-R9AK1OFKw-QCWyRdWyn_DB38dbk7THFHdfQRoCPWcQAvD_BwE.

22   "Katrina Impacts," Hurricans: Science and Society, accessed June 17, 2020, http://www.hurricanescience.org/history/studies/katrinacase/impacts/ .

23   "Passive income is income resulting from cash flow received on a regular basis, requiring minimal to no effort by the recipient to maintain it," The Capital Group Blog, accessed June 17, 2020, https://capitalgroupinsurance.com/passive-income-is-income-resulting-from-cash-flow-received-on-a-regular-basis-requiring-minimal-to-no-effort-by-the-recipient-to-maintain-it/.

24 Debra Bassert. "NAHB Report: Diversifying Housing Options". Opticos, accessed June 17, 2020, https://opticosdesign.com/work/nahb-report-diversifying-housing-options/ .

25 Lynn Richards. "What is Missing Middle Housing?" Missing Middle Housing, accessed June 17, 2020, https://missingmiddlehousing.com .

26 Emma Woolley. "Are tiny houses being used in Canada as social housing?" Homeless Hub, Aparil 8, 2016, https://www.homelesshub.ca/blog/are-tiny-houses-being-used-canada-social-housing.

27   Home Page, Yes in My Backyard, accessed June 17, 2020, http://www.yesinmybackyard.ca/.

28 Elizabet Winkler. "'Snob zoning' is racial housing segregation by another name". The Washington Post, September 25, 2017, https://www.washingtonpost.com/

news/wonk/wp/2017/09/25/snob-zoning-is-racial-housing-segregation-by-another-name/ .

29 Jeff Andrews. "Oregon just effectively banned single-family zoning," Curbed, July 1, 2019, https://www.curbed.com/2019/7/1/20677502/oregon-yimby-single-family-zoning-nimby-rent-control.

30 "Housing Choices (House Bill 2001)", Urban Planning, Department of Land Conservation and Development, Oregon.gov, accessed June 17, 2020, https://www.oregon.gov/lcd/UP/Pages/Housing-Choices.aspx .

31 Ibid.

32 Emily Badger and Quoctrung Bui. "Cities Start to Question an American Ideal: A House with a Yard on Every Lot," The New York Times, June 18, 2019, https://www.nytimes.com/interactive/2019/06/18/upshot/cities-across-america-question-single-family-zoning.html.

33 Ibid.

34 Mike Albanese. "Pushing Back Against the Banning of Single Family Zoning," M Report, November 7, 2019, https://themreport.com/daily-dose/11-07-2019/pushing-back-against-the-banning-of-single-family-zoning.

35 Emily Badger and Quoctrung Bui. "Cities Start to Question an American Ideal: A House with a Yard on Every Lot," The New York Times, June 18, 2019, https://www.nytimes.com/interactive/2019/06/18/upshot/cities-across-america-question-single-family-zoning.html.

36 Ibid.

37 Chris Nichols. "Demonstrators protest SB50 as California Lawmakers Reintroduce Controversial Housing Law," CapRadio, January 7, 2020, https://www.capradio.org/articles/2020/01/07/demonstrators-protest-sb50-as-california-lawmakers-reintroduce-controversial-housing-law/.

38 Marisa Kendall. "Moms4Housing Takes Over Press Conference Announcing New Housing Bill," The Mercury News, January 7, 2020, https://www.mercurynews.com/2020/01/07/moms-4-housing-takes-over-press-conference-announcing-new-housing-bill/.

39 Marisa Endicott. "California's Controversial Housing Bill Just Died. It Wasn't Because of the NIMBYs," Mother Jones, January 30, 2020, https://www.motherjones.com/politics/2020/01/california-housing-bill-sb50-failed-nimby-housing-justice-advocates/.

40 Chris Nichols. "Demonstrators protest SB50 as California Lawmakers Reintroduce Controversial Housing Law," CapRadio, January 7, 2020, https://www.capradio.org/articles/2020/01/07/demonstrators-protest-sb50-as-california-lawmakers-reintroduce-controversial-housing-law/.

41 Chris Nichols. "Demonstrators Protest SB50 As California Lawmakers Reintroduce Controversial Housing Law," CAPRadio, January 7, 2020, https://www.capradio.org/articles/2020/01/07/demonstrators-protest-sb50-as-california-lawmakers-reintroduce-controversial-housing-law/ .

42 Chris Nichols. "Fact or Fiction? A Look At Claims About SB 50, One Of California's Most Controversial Housing Bills," PolitiFact, January 21, 2020,

https://www.politifact.com/article/2020/jan/21/fact-or-fiction-look-claims-about-one-californias-/.

43   Emily Badger and Quoctrung Bui. "Cities Start to Question an American Ideal: A House with a Yard on Every Lot," The New York Times, June 18, 2019, https://www.nytimes.com/interactive/2019/06/18/upshot/cities-across-america-question-single-family-zoning.html.

44   Ed Zotti. "Toronto is close to topping Chicago as North America's second city for skyscrapers. Here's why," Chicago Sun-Times, updated June 15, 2020, https://chicago.suntimes.com/crossroads/2020/6/12/21278779/toronto-skyscrapers-global-cities-chicago-city-crossroads-ed-zotti.

45   Hon. Rick Bartolucci. "Bill 140, Strong Communities through Affordable Housing Act, 2011," Legislative Assembly of Ontario, accessed June 17, 2020, https://www.ola.org/en/legislative-business/bills/parliament-39/session-2/bill-140 .

46   Jennifer Pagliaro and Tess Kalinowski. "What we know and don't know about Ontario's massive new housing law," The Star, May 2, 2019, https://www.thestar.com/news/city_hall/2019/05/02/what-we-know-and-dont-know-about-ontarios-massive-new-housing-law.html .

47   Tess Kalinowski. "Why it's so hard to get housing in Toronto's "yellowbelt" neighborhoods—and how experts say it can be done," The Star, March 16, 2019, https://www.thestar.com/business/real_estate/2019/03/16/why-its-so-hard-to-get-housing-into-torontos-yellowbelt-neighbourhoods-and-how-experts-say-it-can-be-done.html .

48   Emily Badger and Quoctrung Bui. "Cities Start to Question an American Ideal: A House With a Yard on Every Lot," The New York Times, June 18, 2019, https://www.nytimes.com/interactive/2019/06/18/upshot/cities-across-america-question-single-family-zoning.html .

49   Alexander Tanzi. "New York City's Population Is Shrinking: Demographic Trends," Bloomberg, April 18, 2019, https://www.bloomberg.com/news/articles/2019-04-18/new-york-city-s-population-is-shrinking-demographic-trends .

50   Dave Fidlin. "New York population shrinking, graying, Census Bureau data shows," The Center Square, June 25, 2020, https://www.thecentersquare.com/new_york/new-york-population-shrinking-graying-census-bureau-data-shows/article_495ad37a-b666-11ea-8e12-5799d144382e.html .

51   Ibid.

ABOUT THE AUTHOR

Michael did everything he was supposed to do. He fought his way through his schooling, wound up with a Bachelor of Commerce degree, then got a responsible job, met a girl, got married, bought a single family home, and had a child. As he approached 40, he came to the realization that he was stuck in a rat race of long commutes, a dead end job, a failing marriage and endless debt.

By taking control of his future, and building a stream of appreciating, cash-flow generating assets, Michael started to see real changes in his net worth and his mindset.

Resisting every urge to make things more complicated than it needed to be, Michael focused on acquiring simple quality homes with additional dwelling units, then when he could afford it, would do it again. As an investment realtor, he taught others to follow that path to success.

Real estate investing has allowed Michael to do the things he WANTS to do rather than the things he has to do. Whether it be following his beloved LA Dodgers, playing with his dog, spending time with friends and family, scrapbooking, watching classic movies or travelling the world, the goal is to enjoy life and to create as many once in a lifetime experiences as he can.

Today, when he is not sitting back, with his feet up and beverage in hand, in his favorite armchair, you can find Michael continuing to teach others about a simple buy and hold investment strategy, helping them build their wealth so they can experience the choices and financial freedom they desire. Of course, don't be surprised if even then, he's chillaxing by the beach or cruising in his convertible.

Made in the USA
Las Vegas, NV
13 May 2021